CULTURES OF THE WORLD
Guyana

Cavendish
Square

New York

Published in 2020 by Cavendish Square Publishing, LLC
243 5th Avenue, Suite 136, New York, NY 10016
Copyright © 2020 by Cavendish Square Publishing, LLC

Third Edition

Library of Congress Cataloging-in-Publication Data

Names: Jermyn, Leslie, author. | Wong, Winnie, author. | Nevins, Debbie, author.
Title: Guyana / Leslie Jermyn, Winnie Wong, and Debbie Nevins.
Description: Third edition. | New York : Cavendish Square, [2020] |
Series: Cultures of the world | Includes bibliographical references and index.
Identifiers: LCCN 2018057391 (print) | LCCN 2018057966 (ebook) |
ISBN 9781502647474 (ebook) | ISBN 9781502647467 (library bound)
Subjects: LCSH: Guyana--Civilization--Juvenile literature. |
Guyana--Social life and customs--Juvenile literature. |
Guyana--History--Juvenile literature.
Classification: LCC F2368.5 (ebook) | LCC F2368.5 .J47 2020 (print) |
DDC 988.1--dc23
LC record available at https://lccn.loc.gov/2018057391

Writers, Leslie Jermyn, Winnie Wong; Debbie Nevins, third edition
Editorial Director, third edition: David McNamara
Editor, third edition: Debbie Nevins
Art Director, third edition: Alan Sliwinski
Designer, third edition: Jessica Nevins
Production Manager, third edition: Karol Szymczuk
Cover Picture Researcher: Alan Sliwinski
Picture Researcher, third edition: Jessica Nevins

CONTENTS

GUYANA TODAY **5**

1. GEOGRAPHY
Geographic regions • Rivers • Climate • Flooding • Plants and animals • Cities and towns **11**

2. HISTORY
The precolonial period • European discovery and early relations • Plantation society • Fighting for control • Nineteenth century • Pre-independence • After independence • Twenty-first century **23**

3. GOVERNMENT
The constitution • Government structure • The judiciary • The military **35**

4. ECONOMY
Two paths to development • Recent economic trends • Main industries • The workforce • Trade • Transportation **43**

5. ENVIRONMENT
Causes and effects of pollution • Climate change impacts • Deforestation • Wildlife protection • Ecotourism • Waste treatment **51**

6. GUYANESE
Ethnic groups • Population patterns • Ethnic tensions • Guyanese diaspora **61**

7. LIFESTYLE
Marriage and family structure • Rural versus urban living • Housing • Education and literacy • Health **71**

8. RELIGION The main formal religions • Cult groups • Church and state • Folk beliefs **83**

9. LANGUAGE Guyanese Creole • Other languages • Folk wisdom and proverbs • The media **95**

10. ARTS Visual arts • Architecture • Music • Dance • Crafts • Literature **103**

11. LEISURE Making life • Sports **113**

12. FESTIVALS Christian festivals • Hindu festivals • Muslim festivals • Historic holidays **119**

13. FOOD Amerindian traditions • Something for (and from) everyone • Other foods • Drinks • Shopping **125**

MAP OF GUYANA **133**

ABOUT THE ECONOMY **135**

ABOUT THE CULTURE **137**

TIMELINE **138**

GLOSSARY **140**

FOR FURTHER INFORMATION **141**

BIBLIOGRAPHY **142**

INDEX **143**

GUYANA TODAY

LOCATED ON THE NORTHERN COAST OF SOUTH AMERICA, GUYANA is a relatively small country. Nestled between Suriname and Venezuela to its east and west, it also borders the gigantic country of Brazil to the south. Guyana is a country that doesn't often make international headlines, but today it is perched upon the brink of great new possibilities. For better or for worse, they could change everything.

The Cooperative Republic of Guyana was once known as British Guiana. In those days, 1814—1966, it was a British colony and part of the British West Indies. Today, though, it's an independent nation, and the only English-speaking country in South America. In 2016, it celebrated its fiftieth anniversary of independence with a colorful, upbeat, six-week-long festival. Guyanese are naturally proud of their country, poor though it is. In fact, it's the poorest country on the continent and one of the poorest in the Western Hemisphere.

With its natural attributes and resources, Guyana's poverty can seem surprising. After all, this is a land of massive, pristine rain forests endowed with energetic rivers,

Orinduik Falls on the Ireng River is one of Guyana's many impressive waterfalls.

breathtaking waterfalls, and diverse Amazonian wildlife. Bauxite, gold, and diamonds are found beneath its soils. Sugarcane and rice grow in abundance.

But against this backdrop of a rugged and unspoiled ecosystem, Guyana's history is filled with struggles and pain. Caribbean Amerindians, European colonial masters, African slaves, and indentured laborers from East India, China, and Portugal have all left their marks on Guyana. Today their descendents number fewer than one million. Most live along the narrow coastal strip facing the Atlantic Ocean.

Often called the "land of six peoples," the Guyanese are a multiethnic mix. Despite their claims of unity, however, they are divided by racial and ethnic tensions. The Afro-Guyanese and Indo-Guyanese are the largest groups and have most of the political power. They are distinct populations who mostly do not intermix. A racial atmosphere clouds all aspects of society and politics.

The main political parties are dominated by the two groups, and party loyalty depends less on political philosophies than on ethnic makeup. Presidential elections usually pit the candidates of the Indo-Guyanese People's Progressive Party (PPP) against those of the Afro-Guyanese People's National Congress

(PNC). In 2015, David A. Granger, a politician with African roots, became the president with the support of a coalition party which included the PNC. He was to remain Guyana's president until the next elections in 2020, but a vote of no confidence dissolved his government in late 2018. Earlier that year, the seventy-three-year-old president announced that he had been diagnosed with cancer. His illness, non-Hodgkin lymphoma, is a cancer that originates in the lymphatic system. In October of that year, Granger flew to Cuba for more complete testing and to begin chemotherapy treatment.

That the president felt he could not obtain optimal medical treatment in his own country speaks volumes about Guyana. It is a very poor country, and the reasons for that are complicated. It also suffers a severe "brain drain" as educated and highly trained people emigrate abroad in record numbers. They leave behind an inadequate, understaffed, and underfunded health-care system. The problem is circular. Because Guyana is a poor country, homegrown professionals move to other countries for better salaries and better working conditions. In turn, the deficit of skilled workers only reinforces Guyana's poverty.

David A. Granger became the president of the Republic of Guyana in 2015.

Guyana has tried a variety of governing and economic approaches. It had a state-led socialist dictatorship for its first few decades, and moved on to a democratic government with more of a private-sector economy. The latter approach has led to a much improved economy in recent years. Nevertheless, the country is still dragged down by its previously incurred debts, a shortage of skilled labor, deficient infrastructure, and ongoing racial and ethnic tensions.

But wait! A powerful and surprising factor has recently been thrown into this logjam. And it has the potential to blow that logjam wide open. Essentially, Guyana has hit the jackpot, and that jackpot is oil. The big question now is: will the country go boom or bust?

In 2015, the ExxonMobil Corporation and its international partners discovered vast oil reserves off the coast of Guyana. Since then, they have been rapidly building wells. The oil is expected to start flowing in 2020, and ExxonMobil has promised about half the profits to Guyana. That money could be enough to transform the nation into a new international powerhouse, raking in wealth it never imagined. The gush of oil dollars will begin pumping about $300 million each year into the government's coffers, and could rise to $5 billion per year in about ten years.

"This is the best thing that has ever happened to Guyana," said Minister of Finance Winston Jordan in an interview with *Foreign Policy* magazine. Some analysts have breathlessly called the ExxonMobil project "one of the most lucrative new energy discoveries in the world."

But not everyone is happy. Some people in Guyana worry about the natural environment. What if there's an oil spill, like the one that occurred off the coast of Louisiana in 2010? Arguing that the Guyanese government granted the drilling licenses illegally, a group of concerned citizens is suing ExxonMobil and two other oil companies to stop the project. They claim that by failing to obtain the necessary environmental permits, the oil companies are acting illegally.

Another concern, expressed by numerous international publications, is that Guyana won't be able to handle the windfall. After all, it has never been an oil-producing nation. Other resource-rich but poor countries—for example, Venezuela—provide cautionary examples. Mismanagement plus enormous amounts of money can easily result in high-end corruption. Countries like Guyana, with weak governments, ethnic strife, and a general lack of transparency and accountability, often have a poor record of navigating the pitfalls of sudden wealth. This bonanza may well lead to greater inequality in Guyana, with the rich getting richer and the poor getting poorer. The worst-case scenario—armed conflict within the country—is also quite possible.

Naturally, the Guyanese government wants to avoid a bad outcome. As of 2018, officials are taking steps to get the necessary groundwork in place. The challenges are enormous and the odds not all that good. But if Guyana can get it right, all its citizens will benefit. They will enjoy better schools, health care, and infrastructure. Maybe the country's educated professionals will even stay home and help their country be the best it can be. The world is watching with fingers crossed, hoping for this fairy tale to have a happy ending.

Will the discovery of oil reserves off the coast of Guyana lead to the average citizen having more cash in hand?

GEOGRAPHY

The Potaro River flows through the Guyana rain forest.

THE COOPERATIVE REPUBLIC OF Guyana (gee-AH-nah), or Guyana for short, is one of three small countries located in the northeast of the South American continent. The country has an area of 83,000 square miles (214,969 square kilometers), about the same size as Great Britain or slightly smaller than Idaho.

Guyana is bounded on the north by the tropical Atlantic Ocean, on the southeast by Suriname, on the south and southwest by Brazil, and on the northwest by Venezuela.

The capital city, Georgetown, is located on the Atlantic coast. Guyana is a tropical country with rainy and dry seasons, and with minor seasonal temperature change. Several important rivers flow across a land that is rich in plant and animal life.

GEOGRAPHIC REGIONS

Guyana is part of a large region known as the Guianas (gee-AH-nahs) that also includes the countries of Suriname and French Guiana. In the late seventeenth and eighteenth centuries, eastern Venezuela and northern Brazil were part of the Guianas as well. The region is characterized by great river systems and high annual rainfall. The country can be divided into five main natural zones—the coastal plain, the white sand belt, and the interior highlands, which include the rain forests, the dryer savanna regions, and the mountains.

1

The name Guyana is derived from *guiana*, an Amerindian word meaning "land of many waters." With its many rivers, extraordinary waterfalls, and Atlantic Ocean coastline, Guyana lives up to its name.

THE COASTAL PLAIN This narrow strip of land bordering the Atlantic Ocean is where most of Guyana's people live. The coastal region stretches 285 miles (459 kilometers) from Venezuela to Suriname and varies in width from 10 miles (16 km) up to 40 miles (64 km) along major rivers. Although this zone represents only 4—5 percent of total land area, it is very fertile. That's because the soil is made up mostly of mud and silt that has been picked up and swept along by the mighty Amazon River as it wends its way through the northern part of the South American continent. The river empties into the Atlantic in eastern Brazil, and washes the sediment out to sea. From there, this material is carried north by ocean currents and deposited on the shores of Guyana as a rich, fertile clay. The arable coastal region is where the country's two main crops, sugarcane and rice, are intensely cultivated.

Guyana has no well-defined shoreline or sandy beaches. As the land approaches the ocean, it gradually loses elevation until it turns into marshy lowlands, full of swamps. Then, as the land reaches into the sea, it becomes a region of mud flats, shallow brown waters, and sandbars, all of which create barriers to shipping. Off the port town of New Amsterdam, for example, the mud flats extend almost 16 miles (25 km) into the sea. Because ships cannot get close enough to the shore, incoming vessels must partially unload their cargoes offshore in order to reach the docks.

Moving inland, a line of swamps forms a barrier between the coastal plain and the white sandy hills of the interior. These swamps were formed when a series of dams were built on the major rivers and water was prevented from flowing onto coastal croplands. Now the swamps serve as reservoirs during periods of drought. A series of canals separates the swampy areas from the coastal plain.

THE WHITE SAND BELT About 40 miles (64 km) inland, the land rises up into a terrain of low hills, about 90 to 155 miles (150 to 250 km) wide. These white sandy hills, are interspersed with rocky outcroppings and contain most of Guyana's mineral deposits of bauxite, gold, and diamonds. The white sand itself is mostly pure quartz. In some areas, the sands support a dense hardwood forest, but they cannot support crops. Without the trees to hold the soil in place, the land is rapidly eroded.

Guyana boasts of some of the highest and most beautiful waterfalls in the world. Kaieteur Falls, on the Potaro River, is a spectacular 822 feet (251 meters) high. It consists of two falls, a small one of 81 feet (25 m) and a larger one of 820 feet (250 m). By comparison, Niagara Falls—located between the borders of Ontario, Canada, and New York—is only 193 feet (59 m) high. Kaieteur Falls is a major tourist attraction because of its sheer size and the beautiful prismatic colors that form with the mist rising off the water. It is also home to martins and swallows that nest behind the curtain of water; they can be seen swooping home after foraging for food in the surrounding forests.

The name Kaieteur comes from an indigenous language and means "Old Man's Fall." Legend has it that an old chieftain offered himself to the Great Spirit for the good of his people. He paddled his canoe over the edge of the falls and was turned to stone. It is said that you can see his stone canoe when there is a drought and the water level is low. Despite the magnificent size of Kaieteur, it is not the biggest waterfall in Guyana. Two other falls are higher—King George VI Falls on the Utshi River, at 1,600 feet (488 m), and King Edward Falls on the Semang River, at 840 feet (256 m). However, these are not popular tourist attractions because they are hard to reach. Many of Guyana's rivers have smaller falls and rapids that are more accessible from the coast, such as Orinduik Falls on the Ireng River at the Brazilian border.

THE INTERIOR HIGHLANDS Covering over 66,000 square miles (170,940 sq km), the forest zone makes up the largest portion of the country and stretches from the coastal zone to the interior. As the name implies, it is heavily forested. Few people live here because the soil, which is made up of brown and white sands and clays, is not suitable for growing food crops. The land in this zone rises gently from sea level, and the area is crisscrossed with large rivers that empty into the Atlantic Ocean.

The forested regions of the Rupununi are sparsely populated and provide a haven for rare species of birds.

THE SAVANNA ZONE The savanna zone is an area of high grasslands located in the far southwest of the country near the border with Brazil. The largest savanna area is called Rupununi, after the river of the same name that runs through the region. Totaling about 5,792 square miles (15,000 sq km), the Rupununi Savanna is divided in half by the Kanuku Mountains.

The area is sparsely settled, although some Guyanese have cattle ranches there, and a few indigenous groups make their homes on the savanna. There is a second, smaller savanna approximately 100 miles (161 km) southeast of Georgetown. Located in the Upper Berbice River, the Intermediate Savanna consists of 615,000 acres (248,882 hectares) of grass terrain with forestlands dissected by numerous rivers and streams.

THE MOUNTAINS Along the borders with Venezuela and Brazil are the Pakaraima Mountains. This area is characterized by sharply stepped plateaus rising from the savanna plains below. It is the least-settled and least-known region of Guyana. There are believed to be some gold and diamond deposits in the mountains, but due to the lack of transportation, only a few people from the coast have made the journey to try their luck.

The highest point in this range, and in Guyana, is Mount Roraima at 9,301 feet (2,835 m) high. It is located at the point where Venezuela, Brazil, and Guyana meet. Other mountain ranges in Guyana include the Kanuku Mountains (3,000 feet/914 m), and the Merume Mountains, whose highest peak, Mount Caburai, is 4,806 feet (1,465 m).

RIVERS

The four largest rivers found in Guyana include the Demerara, Essequibo, Courantyne, and Berbice. As these rivers flow from their sources high in the mountains to the ocean, the shift in altitude results in dramatic rapids, cataracts, and waterfalls. Guyana has some of the continent's most spectacular waterfalls, and these are popular tourist destinations.

MYSTERIOUS RORAIMA

Mount Roraima covers parts of Guyana, Venezuela, and Brazil. On the Guyana and Brazilian sides, it's entirely made of enormous sheer cliffs that only the most daring and experienced rock climbers have succeeded in scaling. For everyone else, the mountain is accessible only from Venezuela.

Despite its name, Mount Roraima is actually a mesa or plateau, rather than a mountain. Such a tabletop mountain is called a tepui. *It's part of a vast 200,000-square-mile (518,000 sq km) region of sandstone mesas that covers the western bulge of Guyana (above the "waist" where the country narrows) and parts of Venezuela and Brazil. These plateaus are said to be the remains of a large sandstone deposit that covered this region 1.8 billion years ago. The rock is so old that it predates the time when South America and Africa parted to form separate continents 135 million years ago.*

Over the millennia water erosion from many rivers has carved deep ravines and valleys into the mesas. Roraima is the highest of the plateaus, with an elevation of 9,219 feet (2,8010 m) above sea level, and rising 7,671 feet (2,338 m) above the land it sits on. Its highest point lies in Guyana, where it's also the highest peak of Guyana's Highland Range. In a language of the local indigenous people, its name means "singing of waterfalls." It's an apt description because many streams of water plunge off it to the lowlands below. This region is mostly unexplored because of the difficult terrain.

The first expedition to reach the top of Roraima was led by Everard im Thurn, a British botanist, in 1884. Im Thurn brought back samples of plant life that had never been recorded before. The plateaus are isolated because of their height, and this has allowed plants and animals to evolve and thrive in an ecological niche that is not found anywhere else in the world.

When im Thurn lectured about this isolated region after his return to England, the author Arthur Conan Doyle (the creator of Sherlock Holmes) was inspired to write a novel about an expedition in which prehistoric plants and dinosaurs are discovered living high up on Roraima. The book, called The Lost World, *was published in 1912.*

Today, even with modern technology such as helicopters, much of Roraima's 44 square miles (114 sq km) remains unexplored.

CLIMATE

Because Guyana is situated close to the equator, temperatures are high throughout the year. The average daily temperature is 80 degrees Fahrenheit (27 degrees Celsius), with a range of 74°F to 86°F (23°C to 30°C) between night and day. For most people living on the coast, these temperatures are moderated by the constant northeast trade winds that blow off the Atlantic Ocean.

Four seasons, defined not so much by temperature but by the amount of rainfall, can be distinguished in Guyana. Between mid-April and late July there is heavy rainfall. This is followed by a dry season that lasts until November, when another period of lighter rainfall begins. This third season lasts until February, when there is another dry season.

The average annual rainfall in Guyana is 90 inches (229 centimeters), with a range from a low of 60 inches (152 cm) to a high of 120 inches (305 cm), depending on the area and the year. Even during the dry season, the humidity in the air is very high, averaging about 70 percent. Seasonal drought can occur in July and August when the southeast trade wind bypasses the interior. This wet climate has influenced many aspects of life in Guyana, including crop production, dress, design of houses, and the annual cycle of social events.

FLOODING

Guyana is bordered by the ocean on one side and swamps inland, making it very susceptible to floods. Some of this area would normally lie 4 to 5 feet (1.2 to 1.5 m) below sea level, but it is protected by a complicated system of around 140 miles (225 km) of dikes and seawalls. The coastal zone also has high annual rainfall of 70 to 110 inches (178 to 279 centimeters), which further increases the chances of flooding.

In order to keep the land dry, the Guyanese have built and maintained a complicated system of walls, sluices, and canals to control flooding. The first part of the system is a large seawall that prevents the sea from flooding this part of the shore. The wall is equipped with sluice gates that regulate the outflow of water back to the sea and from inland swamps to the sea. At the rear of the coastal strip is another wall or dam that prevents swamp

While the rivers of Guyana may look inviting for a refreshing swim, it's good to know what lives in those waters before diving in. Many of the river dwellers are huge and dangerous.

One of them is a kind of fish measuring about 7 to 8 feet (2.2 to 2.4 m) in length and weighing about 200 pounds (90.7 kilograms). This is the famous arapaima (ah-rah-PAI-

mah), a freshwater fish related to the salmon. The air-breathing arapaima lives in the rivers of the highlands and savannas and is sought by indigenous people and sportsmen alike. Its flesh is said to be delicious, and its scales are used as nail files or to make a variety of ornaments. Arapaima are hunted with harpoons rather than lines and hooks because the fish are so big and strong they can drag fishermen off the bank of a river. Another freshwater giant is the carnivorous black caiman. This reptile, the world's largest alligator species, can reach over 13 feet (4 m) in length and likes to eat capybaras.

The capybara, or water pig, is the world's largest rodent. It looks like a guinea pig but is the size of a small pig. It lives on the riverbanks and can be found there for much of the

day. Indigenous people hunt capybaras for their meat. The matamata (MAH-tah-mah-tah) turtle lives in rivers and hunts fish by luring them with strange weedlike appendages on its head. A species of eel that carries 500 watts of electric current also inhabits Guyana's waterways.

The anaconda is a type of boa constrictor that prefers to live partly in water. These giants can easily crush a human being, although their usual prey is large animals. The manatee, or sea cow, is a mammal that breathes air through collapsible nostrils and suckles its live-born babies, but never leaves the rivers. A manatee eats only plants and is a docile creature. Measuring up to 7 feet (2.1 m) in length, manatees are probably the inspiration for the mermaid myths started by sailors hundreds of years ago.

water from flooding the settled zone. Between these two dams is a complex network of canals and trenches that move water through the area for irrigation and drainage.

The canals and trenches are of two different levels. The high canals are used for irrigation and transportation, while the low trenches are for drainage. These canals and trenches must be kept clean of silt (fine sand that can clog water systems) and plants. Maintaining the system is the responsibility of both the government and the people. The Public Works Department undertakes major repairs to the canals and trenches, but local communities are responsible for maintaining the sluices and cleaning plant life out of the canals. Without hard work and cooperation, life on the coast would be impossible.

PLANTS AND ANIMALS

Guyana enjoys an extraordinary diversity of plant and animal life. From the sea to the deep Amazon regions, there are different ecosystems that support as many as 1,500 species of plants, 500 birds, and 200 mammals, as well as numerous insects, reptiles, amphibians, and fish.

There are three main types of forests in Guyana—mangrove, hardwood, and tropical. Mangrove forests grow along the boundary between fresh water and salt water and survive in a mixture of the two known as brine. Mangroves can be found behind the settled coastal band in the swampy areas where rivers drain into the sea. From there, inland to the first line of cataracts on the major rivers, lies hardwood forest. Forest trees have adapted to living in sandy soil by extending their roots outward to capture water. Tropical forests extend from the cataracts to the border with Brazil and Venezuela. These are dense forests that have largely escaped commercial logging because of their isolation. Some of the species that can be found there include greenheart, mora, and crabwood. These trees can grow up to hundreds of feet tall. Greenheart is especially valuable because its wood does not rot in seawater and can be used to build docks and wharves.

Notable smaller plants include hundreds of varieties of orchids, some of which have adapted to living in trees with no soil, and the Regis water lily, which lives in freshwater pools. This water lily, which can grow 6 feet (1.8 m) in diameter, is the largest leafed aquatic plant in the world. In the tropical jungle are several types of vines that live suspended from huge trees. The best known of these is the liana vine, a weak tree that grows up the trunk of another in search of sunlight. The bark of a different vine, known locally as *urari* (oo-RAH-ree), is used to make a poison that is more deadly than that of many snakes.

A leaf-cutter ant demonstrates how it got its name.

As a tropical country, Guyana also has many insects, including beautiful jungle butterflies, such as the morpho butterfly, and leaf-cutter ants. The leaf-cutter or parasol ant is a species that grows a type of fungus for food in its underground nests. The fungus needs rotting vegetation to survive, so the leaf-cutters work hard to provide their food with food. They can strip a tree of leaves very quickly.

With so many rivers, it is no surprise that Guyana has an abundance of freshwater fish. Perhaps the most famous Amazon fish is the piranha, with its sharp teeth and carnivorous habits. Some species of piranha attack humans and other large mammals, but most are not meat-eaters. They prefer still pools of water, so many rapids and waterfalls in Guyana are safe. A favorite with sport fishermen is the lukanani (loo-kah-NAH-nee), which resembles the largemouth bass. Another member of Guyana's diverse fish life is the arapaima, which can weigh around 200 pounds (90.7 kg).

Bird life includes dozens of species of hummingbirds with beautiful plumage and a wide array of parrots and macaws. An elusive jungle dweller is the golden cock of the rock (*Rupicola rupicola*). The males are a golden-orange color with a crest that looks like a Roman helmet. They have an unusual mating ritual, where the male bird clears an area of jungle floor and strikes a variety of poses while waiting for the brown-colored female to choose from among the competitors. Some males wait for weeks and are never chosen.

This street scene in Georgetown shows the famous Stabroek Market in the background.

CITIES AND TOWNS

The most heavily populated region is the coast. About 90 percent of the Guyanese live and work there. The other three zones support scattered populations of mostly indigenous people who live off the land.

The capital city, Georgetown, has the largest urban population, at about 200,500. Located at the mouth of the Demerara River, the city was founded by the British in 1781. The Dutch later claimed the settlement, but it was finally won by the British and given its present name in 1812. Georgetown is one of the best examples of a Georgian-style wooden Caribbean city, and it is sometimes called the Garden City of the Caribbean. Many of the colonial buildings have been preserved, as have the large tree-lined avenues built by the Dutch. Other important cities include Linden, 40 miles (64 km) south of Georgetown on the Demerara River, and New Amsterdam, 62 miles (100 km) southeast of Georgetown at the mouth of the Berbice River.

All three cities are important shipment points for Guyana's most valuable mineral, bauxite. Linden and New Amsterdam are considerably smaller than Georgetown, with populations of about 30,000 and 33,000, respectively. There are many other small settlements along the coast but very few inland.

INTERNET LINKS

https://www.arkive.org/black-caiman/melanosuchus-niger
This wildlife site provides a good overview of the black caiman.

https://www.atlasobscura.com/places/mount-roraima
This site offers a slide show of Mount Roraima.

https://www.bradtguides.com/articles/top-natural-attractions -guyana
Kaieteur Falls is among the natural attractions featured on this travel site.

https://www.kaieteurnewsonline.com/category/features -columnists/interesting-creatures-in-guyana
Information about hundreds of Guyana's fascinating creatures are featured on this site, along with photos.

https://www.lonelyplanet.com/the-guianas/guyana/georgetown
This travel site features top spots in Georgetown along with other places of interest in Guyana.

https://www.sciencealert.com/welcome-to-mount-roraima-the -floating-island-plateau
More information and images can be found in this article on Mount Roraima.

HISTORY

This 1888 engraving shows a view of Georgetown as seen from the lighthouse on the Demerara River.

2

GUYANA HAD TWO DIFFERENT colonial masters before independence in 1966, and much of its history has been driven by the demands of these European powers and their desire to gain from their colonies. The aftermath of the colonial history continues to haunt modern Guyana through ethnic politics and discord.

THE PRECOLONIAL PERIOD

Long before Europeans even suspected that the Americas existed, people were already living in the area that became Guyana. These indigenous inhabitants, known today as Amerindians, were largely seminomadic, living in stable settlements for a period of time before moving their villages to new locations. They mainly practiced shifting horticulture, growing staple crops such as cassava in small farm plots, and also hunting and fishing. Most villages consisted of one or two large extended families of fewer than seventy people.

These villages had no formal leaders or chiefs, but important men from each of the families competed to become informal village leaders. When this competition became heated, or when the village grew too large for the farms to support the people, some members moved out to form new settlements. Each village also had a shaman, whose job included curing the sick and maintaining good relations between the people and the spirits and gods. In the Guianas (including present-day Guyana, Suriname, and

Guyana attained unwanted notoriety in 1978 after a cult of US citizens committed mass suicide there, resulting in 918 deaths. Their remote compound in the rain forest, known as Jonestown, has since grown over with jungle, and most Guyanese feel that's just as well. Some, however, would like to turn the infamous site into an attraction for much-needed tourism.

French Guiana), there were several different groups of people. When the first Europeans arrived, they encountered the Carib and Arawak near the coast and the Warrau and Akawáio farther inland.

EUROPEAN DISCOVERY AND EARLY RELATIONS

Since people were already living in Guyana, it is not quite accurate to talk about "discovery" by Europeans as if they were the first inhabitants. Christopher Columbus sailed by the coast of the Guianas on his third voyage in 1498, but did not land there due to the inhospitable appearance of the mangrove forests and swamps along the shore. It was not until nearly a hundred years later that the Dutch, who were then a major commercial power, and English explorers and settlers began to take an interest in the Guianas. The first explorers, the most notable being Sir Walter Raleigh, an English adventurer and writer, brought back stories that inspired both European powers to promote colonization.

The first permanent settlement was founded in 1616 on an island in the estuary of the Essequibo River. It was led by the Dutch but included English settlers as well. This colony expanded to the Demerara River later that century, and a separate Dutch colony was founded on the Berbice River. At

The ruins of Fort Zeelandia on an island in the Essequibo River delta harken back to the earliest Dutch settlement in Guyana.

RALEIGH'S VISION OF GUYANA

Sir Walter Raleigh, better known for his efforts to establish a colony in present-day North Carolina, also explored what later became Guyana. He made two voyages in 1595 and 1617 for Queen Elizabeth I of England, searching for the fabled El Dorado, or land of gold. This was a rumor started around the time of Columbus's early voyages that there existed a land of indigenous people whose capital city was called Manoa. Reportedly, the city and the people were covered with gold. Many adventures began in Europe with the idea of finding this legendary land, and Raleigh believed that it was located inland from the Guianese coast. Although he never found Manoa or El Dorado, his writings about his travels inspired many others to seek their fortunes in the Guianas.

For example, he told prospective explorers that they "shall find there more rich and beautiful cities, more temples adorned with golden images, than either Cortez found in Mexico, or Pizarro in Peru ... Guiana is a country that is still untouched ... The face of the earth is still untorn." In another passage, he described a crystal mountain covered with diamonds where waters fall. The waterfall was described as making the sound of "one thousand great bells ... knocked one against the other." Years later, exploration of the great sandstone plateaus such as Roraima confirmed the story. Waterfalls do indeed cascade over mountains, and sometimes the light does make the sand particles of the rock shine like diamonds!

first Europeans settled the riverbanks far inland and away from the coast. The economy of these early settlements was based on growing tropical crops such as tobacco, cotton, coffee, and cocoa, and on trade with local Amerindian groups for forest products such as annatto (a vegetable dye) and wood from trees. Unlike the Spanish and Portuguese, who established settlements elsewhere on the South American continent, the Dutch maintained friendly relations with the Amerindians and did not use them as slaves.

PLANTATION SOCIETY

Throughout the second half of the 1600s, European settlers began to move toward the coast and away from their riverine farms. At the same time there was an economic shift from crops such as cotton and tobacco toward sugar. The first sugarcane plantation was started in 1658, and throughout the 1700s, the Essequibo and Demerara colonies became more and more dependent on this one crop. The Dutch set out to reclaim coastal swamplands and protected the reclaimed land from the sea by constructing walls and dikes. Once it was fortified, the land was planted with large estates of sugarcane.

Hundreds of thousands of African slaves were brought in to work on sugarcane and cotton plantations in the Americas, and the Dutch plantations were among the worst in terms of the abuse of human rights. The appalling conditions of slavery sparked many minor rebellions as well as a couple of major ones in Guyana. One slave revolt led by Cuffy in 1763 made him a national hero.

First the Dutch, and later the British, relied on the allegiance of Amerindians to help control the African slaves. Amerindians were used as militia, and friendly relations were maintained with them through trade until slavery was ended in 1834.

FIGHTING FOR CONTROL

Toward the end of the eighteenth century, control of the colonies at Essequibo, Demerara, and Berbice shifted several times between the British and the Dutch. The British first seized control of the three colonies in 1781. However, they only held on for a year before the French, allies of the Dutch, took back the colonies and returned them to Dutch control. In 1796, the British captured the colonies again and managed to hold on to them for six years. The Treaty of Amiens, signed in 1802, returned the colonies to the Dutch once again. This treaty held for only one year before the Netherlands and Britain once again went to war and the colonies returned to British control. All this flip-flopping ended in 1814, when the Dutch finally gave the colonies to Britain. Essequibo, Demerara,

LABORING FOR SUGAR

Sugar sustained colonial Guiana and continues to be an important product in the modern economy. The wealth that it generated, however, came at the expense of many thousands of lives lost or lived in poverty and misery—first in slavery and later under the indenture system.

The life of a slave began with capture in West Africa and shipment to the New World in ships designed to hold as many people as possible. If the slave survived this horrifying journey, called "the Middle Passage," he or she would be auctioned off at one of the slave ports in South or North America. From there began a new life of misery.

Slaves on Dutch estates were expected to work a minimum of fourteen hours a day, starting at dawn. They had to work in the sugarcane fields and do any other chores required by the estate master. In addition, they were expected to grow some of their own food at night to supplement the meager rations provided by the owner. Any misbehavior was punishable by the whip and other inhumane tortures such as the amputation of a leg or death by burning over a slow fire. Not surprisingly, many slaves tried to escape or revolt.

Indentured workers, most of them from India, were legally free, unlike slaves, but they also suffered inhumane working and living conditions. From the point at which they signed their contracts in their home countries, their rights were ignored. Contractors often lied about conditions in Guyana to attract workers and even resorted to kidnapping unwilling workers. They, too, were crowded onto ships under unsanitary conditions and left to fend for themselves during the long journey. Some ships had mortality rates of up to 25 percent. Indentured workers were supposed to work a seven- or ten-hour day, depending on whether they were in the fields or the factory, but in reality they often worked eleven to eighteen hours a day. This was hardly any improvement over slavery.

Workers were fined for resisting the system and sometimes beaten and whipped, just as the slaves had been. They received no legal protection from the colonial state and were often arrested or killed when they "rebelled" in an attempt to get justice.

Sugar has much to answer for in the history of Guyana since it forms such a tragic part of the history of both the Afro- and Indo-Guyanese.

The Demerara Rebellion of 1823 was an uprising of more than ten thousand slaves working on sugar plantations.

and Berbice were united in a single colony called British Guiana in 1831.

NINETEENTH CENTURY

The most significant event in Guyana's history during the nineteenth century was the emancipation of the African slaves. British Guiana was then one of the main producers of sugar in the Caribbean region. When the slaves were given their freedom in 1834, many of them decided to leave the estates and work plots of their own land in the towns, and they became the majority urban population. This created a severe labor shortage on the estates, and plantation owners lobbied the British government to find a solution to their problem.

The solution was the indentured labor system. The indenture system worked by contracting laborers in their home countries for a fixed period of work—usually five to seven years—in return for their passage to the country where they would work and either their passage home at the end or the option to stay on in their new country. Wages were fixed and very low, which allowed the plantation owners to continue to produce sugar at competitive prices. Although indentured workers were formally free, the conditions of work were not much of an improvement over slavery.

The first group of laborers brought to Guyana under contract to work for the plantations included the English, Irish, and Germans. This trial lasted only from 1835 to 1839 because northern Europeans were too susceptible to tropical diseases. One group, however, proved to be quite adaptable—the Portuguese. For twenty-seven years, from 1835 to 1862, a total of 31,628 Portuguese workers were brought to British Guiana. When their contracts ended, many stayed on and entered small commercial enterprises. To meet the heavy demand for labor, other countries were targeted by the indenture system—India and China.

At the time of emancipation in 1834, there were 308 sugarcane estates. By 1904, there were only forty-six sugarcane estates. By 1967, there were just eighteen, and fifteen of these sugarcane estates were controlled by a single company—the Booker Brothers Company.

Emancipation meant that sugarcane plantation owners no longer had free labor. Although indentured labor was successfully used, it cost more, and the change from one system to the other forced many smaller plantations out of business. At the same time, people buying sugar in Britain were unhappy about having to pay more for Caribbean sugar in order to protect the plantations there. By 1836, the British government had decided to allow free competition between Caribbean planters and those in India. This also helped cause the failure and collapse of small estates.

Two London-based companies that specialized in the sugar trade were Booker Brothers and John McConnell Company. Both companies benefited when the price of sugar fell in the 1880s; they were able to buy up estates that were no longer profitable. In 1900, the two companies merged to form the Booker Brothers McConnell Company Limited. This commercial giant continued to expand ownership of ever larger estates until it controlled nearly the whole sugar industry.

Booker Brothers, as it was known locally, also expanded into other parts of Guyana's economy. It owned a network of retail stores, the largest taxi service in the country, a pharmaceutical factory, and rum distilleries. It was involved in publishing, advertising, real estate, insurance, cattle ranching, and even owned its own shipping service.

Until independence in 1966, Booker Brothers was the effective power in British Guiana's economy, so much so that the colony was often called "Booker's Guiana."

Chinese indentured laborers began to arrive in 1853. By 1912, this flow of labor was halted, but by then about 14,000 workers had come to British Guiana, and many, like the Portuguese, stayed on and entered commercial trades. But by far the largest group of foreign workers was the East Indians.

The first laborers arrived in 1838. By the time the practice was stopped due to a request from the colonial government in India in 1917, about 238,960 Indians had been transported to British Guiana. They formed the backbone of plantation labor during the nineteenth century and went on to become the majority ethnic group in modern Guyana.

At the end of their work terms, some Indians decided to return home, and 75,547 people were repatriated between 1843 and 1949. Many others stayed on at the estates, and some gave up their right to return passage in order to receive parcels of land and become farmers in their new home. They developed rice agriculture in Guyana and are still the largest ethnic group in rural villages.

The indenture system helped ease the labor shortage, but sugar production never recovered after the slaves were freed. Many small plantations could no longer compete and were bought out by bankers and other plantation owners. The result of this process set the stage for colonial politics in the twentieth century.

PRE-INDEPENDENCE

British Guiana entered the twentieth century with an eighteenth-century form of the colonial government that had been established by the Dutch. The country was effectively controlled by estate owners rather than by the people.

In 1928 Britain reformed the system, abolishing the Dutch-established councils and replacing them with a legislative council. Nevertheless, the first election for the legislative council in which everyone who was twenty-one or older could vote, was not held until 1953.

Meanwhile the general population had become increasingly active in resisting British rule and British companies. The first mass political party, the People's Progressive Party (PPP), was founded in 1950 by Cheddi Jagan, an East Indian dentist, and Forbes Burnham, a British-educated Afro-Guyanese lawyer. Distinctly left-wing, the PPP won the elections of 1953, but the British governor suspended the government, claiming that this was a communist insurgence.

Burnham then broke away to form the People's National Congress (PNC) in 1957. The PPP continued to win subsequent elections despite Britain's intervention, and relations in the colony continued to worsen as numerous labor strikes were violently suppressed by the authorities. Before the 1964 elections, Britain changed the voting rules so that the PPP could not win a majority. Although the PNC also failed to gain a majority, it was able to form a coalition government with the United Force (UF) that largely represented Amerindian and Portuguese interests. Secure that the left-wing PPP was shut out of power, Britain granted Guyana its freedom in 1966.

AFTER INDEPENDENCE

Upon gaining power in the newly independent country, Burnham set out to create a virtual dictatorship with himself and his party at the helm. In 1970 he proclaimed Guyana a cooperative republic and committed the country to a socialist economic path. In the early 1970s, many foreign companies and industries were nationalized as part of this plan.

In 1980, Burnham approved a new constitution that gave the president more power. This constitution also guaranteed the right to work and affirmed the equality of women. The economy was suffering from low prices for its main exports, and there were food shortages and labor unrest. Burnham cracked down on the people and was accused by local and international organizations of rigging the 1980 elections that put him in power once again. Burnham died in August 1985 and was succeeded by Vice President Hugh Desmond Hoyte.

Hoyte led the PNC to victory in the 1985 elections and reversed some of Burnham's policies during his term of office. In 1988, he began to work with the International Monetary Fund (IMF) to renovate Guyana's economy. These changes were part of his Economic Recovery Program (ERP) designed to increase private ownership of businesses and to encourage foreign investment in Guyana. Since the 1985 elections were also questionable, Hoyte agreed to electoral reform and to have international observers, such as the Carter Center of Atlanta, present for the next round of elections. To allow enough time to make necessary changes, elections were postponed from 1990 to 1992.

Much to the dismay of the PNC, Cheddi Jagan and the PPP won the 1992 elections. Jagan set out to revise the constitution to guarantee free elections in the future. He also committed his government to Hoyte's ERP, despite the high cost being paid by Guyana's workers and poor. When Jagan died in March 1997, Vice President Samuel A. Hinds became president until elections in December the same year. The PPP won the elections under their new leader, Janet Jagan, the late Cheddi Jagan's wife.

Since independence Guyana had struggled with a failing economy and political problems. First under Burnham's dictatorship and then under the harsh economic policies of the ERP, the Guyanese have seen both their civil liberties and ability to make a living deteriorate. This has caused massive immigration to countries such as the United States, Canada, and Great Britain, and to other countries in the Caribbean region. The economy began to turn around in 1991, but by then, many educated Guyanese had already established new homes elsewhere.

TWENTY-FIRST CENTURY

The turn of the century brought more problems for Guyana. Bharrat Jagdeo of the PPP became president after Janet Jagan stepped down in 1999, citing ill health. He was reelected in 2001 and again in 2006, but his administration met with protests. Much of the political protest was fueled by ethnic conflict between the mostly Afro-Guyanese PNC and the mostly Indo-Guyanese PPP. The political unrest, in turn, sparked a violent crime wave in 2002 after five convicts broke out of Georgetown Prison.

This upheaval was followed by natural turmoil in 2005, when severe flooding beset the nation. Ordinarily accustomed to about 7 inches (18 cm) of rainfall per month, Guyana experienced excessive downpours from late December 2004 through early February 2005 of up to 40 inches (102 cm)—the most rainfall in more than one hundred years. The deluge killed thirty-four people, destroyed crops and livestock, knocked out water treatment stations, and left more than thirty-five thousand people homeless. Contaminated flood waters were slow to recede and caused unsanitary conditions, leading to the spread of epidemic diseases.

Political unrest continued in the following years, even though the economy had picked up. The presidency of Donald Ramotar, from 2011 to 2015, was fraught with political maneuvering, legislative gridlock, and a shutdown of parliament. The 2015 elections resulted in the former military officer David A. Granger (b. 1945) becoming president, ending more than two decades of rule by the Indian-dominated PPP. He is eligible for one more term if he wins reelection. The next election was to be held in 2020, but after a surprise vote of no confidence in late December 2018, Granger's coalition government fell and new elections were scheduled for March 2019.

In November 2018, the Ministry of the President announced that Granger, age seventy-three, had been diagnosed with non-Hodgkin's lymphoma, a cancer of the lymphatic system. He subsequently received further tests and chemotherapy in Cuba.

In 2007, a longtime maritime border dispute between Guyana and Suriname was settled by a UN tribunal. The intervention was prompted by skirmishes in 2000 between Guyanese oil explorers and Surinamese coast guards. Another border dispute, with Venezuela, was referred to the International Court of Justice in 2018 after a year of talks failed between the two nations. That dispute, over the Essequibo region, dates back more than a century and has been heightened by the discovery of oil in the area. The disputed land, claimed by Venezuela, makes up some two-thirds of present-day Guyana.

INTERNET LINKS

https://www.bbc.com/news/world-latin-america-15799345
This article recounts the Jonestown massacre and looks at what remains there today.

https://www.bbc.com/news/world-latin-america-19546913
The BBC provides a timeline of key events in the history of Guyana.

https://dpi.gov.gy/update-timeline-of-guyana-venezuela-border-controversy
The Guyanese government provides a Guyanese view of the border dispute with Venezuela.

GOVERNMENT

The Parliament Building in Georgetown dates to 1834.

3

T HE COOPERATIVE REPUBLIC OF Guyana is a parliamentary republic with a presidential system. It has both a president and a prime minister. It has been an independent nation since 1966, when it won its freedom from Great Britain, the colonial power that had dominated it for more than 150 years.

After achieving independence, Guyana endured a virtual dictatorship under its second president, Forbes Burnham. Since then, it has seen numerous reforms but also years of political unrest. Nevertheless, the government today is reasonably stable, and power changes hands peacefully according to electoral results.

Guyanese politics is largely based on party allegiance. There are seven political parties, but only two, the People's Progressive Party (PPP) and the People's National Congress (PNC) have been dominant in running the country. Party membership in both cases is open to all, but tends to break along ethnic lines, with the PPP being largely supported by Indo-Guyanese, and the PNC being primarily Afro-Guyanese. In 2011, the coalition A Partnership for National Unity (APNU) was formed. A left-leaning political alliance of the PNC with other groups, it was led by David A. Granger in the 2015 elections. It won those elections by a small margin, making Granger the new president of Guyana.

The country's constitution states, "Guyana is an indivisible, secular, democratic sovereign state in the course of transition from capitalism to socialism and shall be known as the Co-operative Republic of Guyana." Although it is unusual for a constitution to declare that a nation is in a state of transition, the same constitution has been in place since 1980.

THE CONSTITUTION

The constitution is the supreme law of Guyana. The document, first drawn up in 1966 at the time of independence, was replaced in 1980 under Forbes Burnham. In 2001, a new preamble, or introduction, replaced the previous one. The new preamble tones down some of the socialist revolutionary language of the first, and stresses diversity, equality, youth, and environmental responsibility.

GOVERNMENT STRUCTURE

Guyana's government consists of the office of the president and the elected unicameral parliament, the National Assembly.

THE PRESIDENT   The president is the supreme executive authority, head of state, and commander of the armed forces, and is elected for a five-year term. There are no term limits. The president appoints a vice president and prime minister (both titles apply to the same person) from among the elected members of the assembly.

THE PARLIAMENT   Guyana's government consists of the office of the president and the elected unicameral National Assembly, which has sixty-five members. Out of those, forty are elected directly by proportional representation at the national level. The other twenty-five are elected at the regional level—in other words, each of the ten regions elects a certain number of representatives to parliament.

Anyone who is at least eighteen years of age, has Guyanese citizenship, and lives in the country on election day is eligible to vote. For all the elected seats in the National Assembly, people vote for a party rather than for an individual. The party that wins the largest number of seats forms the government.

In addition to these elected members, nonelected Guyanese may also play important roles in government. The speaker of the house, for example, is chosen by the assembly on the first day of a new government, but may not be one of the elected representatives. If the speaker is chosen from outside,

Janet Rosenberg (1920–2009) was an American Jewish girl who married an Indo-Guyanese man named Cheddi Jagan (1918–1997). She came to British Guiana in December 1943 and became involved in the labor struggle, working with labor hero Hubert Nathaniel Critchlow. She and her husband founded the left-wing People's Progressive Party (PPP),

and she became active in politics and government. She served as Guyana's first lady when Cheddi Jagan became president in 1992. After her husband's death, she became Guyana's first woman president in 1997, but she resigned after twenty months due to ill health.

She authored several publications on the history of the PPP. There are also five children's storybooks to her credit, including When Grandpa Cheddi Was a Boy, Children's Stories of Guyana's Freedom Struggles, *and* Alligator Ferry Service. *Janet Jagan received the Mahatma Gandhi Gold Medal in recognition of her struggle for peace, democracy, and women's rights from UNESCO in 1997.*

he or she loses the power to cast tie-breaking votes. The president can also choose additional vice presidents, ministers, and members of his cabinet from outside the group of elected representatives. These people become part of the government, but they do not vote in the National Assembly. The president also chooses the leader of the opposition from among the elected representatives.

To vote a bill into law, one-third of the assembly must be present, and the majority must agree. The approved bill then passes to the president. If the

The flag of Guyana, which was adopted in 1966, has a green background with a white-bordered yellow triangle from side to side, superimposed with a black-bordered red triangle half the size of the yellow one. All the colors have significance for the country and its people. Red represents the people's energy in building a new country, while black represents perseverance. Mineral wealth and the country's forward thrust are represented by yellow, and its rivers by white. Green represents the economic resources of agriculture and forests. The white border symbolizes the rivers.

The coat of arms was also adopted in 1966 and includes symbols that represent people, nature, and history: an Amerindian headdress representing the indigenous people of the country; two diamonds representing mining; a helmet representing the monarchy (of Great Britain); a shield decorated with the national flower, the Regis water lily; two jaguars holding a pickax, sugarcane, and rice to symbolize labor and the main agricultural industries; three wavy blue lines representing Guyana's many waterways; and a Canje pheasant representing the national bird.

The motto of the country is "One People, One Nation, One Destiny."

president chooses, he or she may reject the bill and send it back to the assembly for revision. The assembly can then change the bill according to presidential instructions or, with a two-thirds majority, send the bill back to the president for approval. In such a case, the president must sign the bill into law within twenty-one days or dissolve the assembly. In the case of dissolution, elections must be called immediately. Although the president of Guyana is powerful, he or she cannot veto a bill approved by the majority of the National Assembly.

Local government is administered by the regional councils, whose members are also elected for five-year terms. They can be dissolved by the president before the end of their term. Large cities, such as Georgetown, have elected city councils as well.

City Hall in Georgetown is a Gothic Revival building dating to 1889. It's often called the prettiest building in Georgetown.

THE JUDICIARY

The Supreme Court of Judicature in Guyana consists of the Court of Appeal, the High Court, and a number of courts of summary jurisdiction. The High Court has jurisdiction over all civil matters that are referred to it by local magistrates. It has limited powers in criminal matters. Appeals are taken to either the Court of Appeal or the High Court, with right of final appeal to the Caribbean Court of Justice. The chief justice is head of the High Court and is a member of the Court of Appeal.

THE MILITARY

The Guyana Defense Force (GDF) has about eighty thousand members. It has its origin in the Special Service Unit (SSU), which started under the British as an internal security force. Under Forbes Burnham, the SSU was converted to Guyana's army, navy, and air force, and leadership was given to black officers. In this way, the GDF was used more to contain resistance to Burnham's dictatorship than to protect Guyana's borders.

Both Guyana and Venezuela claim a large section of the Guiana Highlands, of which Mount Roraima is a part. This geological formation contains minerals such as bauxite, nickel, and manganese, as well as iron, diamonds, and gold, and this wealth is the reason both parties have persevered for so long. Constituting about three-fifths of Guyana's current territory, the disputed area involves land west of the Essequibo River.

The dispute started in the nineteenth century when the British claimed the territory for themselves. Venezuela had controlled it, but lost control when its outposts were closed due to civil war in the early 1800s. The British sent in an expedition to mark the border in 1844, and from that point on, Venezuela disputed the new international border. Venezuela asked the British to agree to abide by the decision of an international tribunal, but until the United States became involved in the 1890s, the British refused. Finally bowing to international pressure, the British agreed to the tribunal. The tribunal's decision, which favored the British claim, was issued on October 3, 1899, in Paris, in an agreement since known as the Paris Tribunal. Everything seemed to be settled until 1944, when one of the members of the tribunal died, leaving behind a confidential document arguing that the tribunal had been biased in favor of the British. Once again matters heated up.

When Guyana gained its independence, the new government, along with the British and the Venezuelans, committed itself to trying to find a peaceful settlement. Venezuela ignored this agreement when it occupied Ankoko Island in 1966. By 1970, in order to avoid making the crisis worse, Venezuela and Guyana agreed to do nothing further for twelve years in a document known as the Port of Spain Protocol. When this period expired in 1982, the Venezuelans refused to renew it, thus opening talks once again. At that point the matter was referred to the United Nations (UN) for settlement.

In 2018, after UN brokered discussions between the two nations failed to produce any progress after a year of talks, the matter was refered to the International Court of Justice.

Further disputes between the two countries have arisen in recent years regarding maritime claims. In 2015, exploration in disputed waters by the US oil company Exxon (granted a license to drill by Guyana) indicated the presence of oil. This claim has since exacerbated the territorial tensions between Guyana and Venezuela.

The Guyana Police Force is similarly predominantly black and was also used by Burnham to protect his position. A paramilitary force called the Guyana National Service (GNS), which was made up of young people about to enter college, was dissolved by Bharrat Jagdeo's administration. Instead of serving one year of national service in remote areas of the country before beginning their studies, they are being trained in entrepreneurial skills to become businesspeople.

INTERNET LINKS

https://www.cia.gov/library/PUBLICATIONS/the-world-factbook/geos/gy.html
The CIA World Factbook provides up-to-date information about Guyana's government.

https://freedomhouse.org/report/freedom-world/2018/guyana
A thorough overview of political rights and civil liberties in Guyana is provided on this site.

https://www.nytimes.com/2015/11/19/world/americas/in-guyana-a-land-dispute-with-venezuela-escalates-over-oil.html
This article examines the long-simmering land dispute between Guyana and Venezuela.

http://parliament.gov.gy
This is the official website of the Parliament of Guyana, which includes a PDF of the constitution.

ECONOMY

The Guyanese $20 bill is the lowest denomination of the country's paper currency. Coins are issued in $10, $5, and $1 amounts.

4

RICE, SUGAR, GOLD, BAUXITE, shrimp, and timber—these are the resources that Guyana depends on most to build its economy. The nation is trying to climb out of a deep economic hole that was dug several decades ago by misguided leadership, with policies that resulted in impoverishment. Although the future looks brighter now than it has for many years, the people continue to struggle to make ends meet in this very poor country.

In January 2018, an estimated 3.2 billion barrels of oil were found off the coast of Guyana. The country is on track to become a petroleum producer by 2020.

TWO PATHS TO DEVELOPMENT

From 1970 on, President Forbes Burnham instituted a number of major economic reforms, changing the British system. He renamed Guyana a cooperative republic. His goal was to create a socialist economy in which major industries were owned and run on a cooperative basis. This meant that there could be no foreign ownership, so Burnham set out to nationalize the country's main foreign-controlled companies. The biggest were the Booker Brothers' sugar interests, the Demerara Bauxite Company (owned by Canada's ALCAN), and American-owned Reynolds Mines (also

Bauxite has long been important to Guyana's economy. This bauxite-producing plant was photographed in 1972.

a bauxite mining interest). Besides sugar and bauxite, Burnham also created a number of government-owned enterprises to produce or manage every other aspect of the economy, and he nationalized twenty-nine other companies.

By 1975 Guyana was facing economic difficulty when the prices for both bauxite and sugar declined on the world market. Burnham borrowed money to keep the economy going, but this only increased Guyana's foreign debt. Inflation ballooned, and by 1989, four years after Burnham's death, Guyana had replaced Haiti as the poorest country in the Western Hemisphere.

After coming into office as Burnham's successor, Desmond Hoyte began to negotiate with international agencies such as the World Bank and the International Monetary Fund (IMF) to restructure the economy and renegotiate the country's debt. In 1988, Hoyte introduced the Economic Recovery Program (ERP), which reversed Burnham's policies. Under the ERP, Guyana began to encourage foreign investment and sold some government companies to private owners. For example, a new bauxite mine was opened in Aroima with Reynolds, and a gold mine concession on the Omai River was granted to foreign companies.

One of the demands of the IMF was that the government had to reduce expenses. As a result, many government workers lost their jobs. Guyana was also forced to allow its currency, the Guyana dollar, to "float"—that is, let it reflect the true strength of the Guyanese economy on the world market.

A devaluation of the currency effectively occurred; more and more dollars were needed to buy the same amount of foreign goods. Many of the world's poorer and indebted nations have had to go through these changes, which are called "structural adjustment." Although structural adjustment improves production, exports, and the government's ability to pay its debts, it does not improve the lives of the people. The Guyanese saw their standard of living plummet, as a result of high unemployment and inflation. This prompted massive immigration in the late 1980s and early 1990s.

RECENT ECONOMIC TRENDS

All this may seem like ancient history, but the effects of those years are still being felt in the Guyanese economy today. The policies of the 1970s and 1980s left the Guyanese government heavily in debt to outside lenders. Those debts carried forward into the twenty-first century, and the serious financial burden prevented Guyana from investing in growth-oriented public projects. A government in that condition also has a hard time attracting foreign investment.

Guyana joined the CARICOM (Caribbean Community) Single Market and Economy in 2006. This enabled the country to broaden its export market, primarily in the raw materials sector (naturally occurring resources such as metals and timber). Guyana has experienced positive growth almost every year over the past decade.

In recent years, the government has also significantly reduced its debts. In 2007, the Inter-American Development Bank, Guyana's primary donor, canceled Guyana's nearly $470 million debt, equivalent to 21 percent of GDP. That, along with other debt forgiveness measures, had greatly improved Guyana's situation by 2017.

Much of Guyana's economic growth in recent years has come from a surge in gold production. In 2016, the country produced a record-breaking amount of gold, such that gold production offset the economic effects of declining sugar production.

MAIN INDUSTRIES

AGRICULTURE   Agriculture is the biggest sector of the economy. The narrow coastal zone supports sugarcane and rice, which together account for most of Guyana's agricultural exports. The Guyana Sugar Corporation (GuySuCo), established in 1976, is the largest employer in Guyana and the Caribbean, with some seventeen thousand workers. It produces high-quality brown Demerara sugar and molasses. Most of the sugar is exported to Europe, and the molasses is sold to local rum distilleries. It also sells sugar to neighboring CARICOM countries, and to a lesser extent, to North America.

Rice is the second most important agricultural product. Most rice is grown along the coastal areas, though there are paddies in other areas, particularly in the Upper Takutu—Upper Essequibo region in the south. Guyana produces two rice crops per year. In 2017—2018, Guyana's rice growers enjoyed a higher than expected production of about 1,022,945 tons (928,000 metric tons), about 8 percent higher than in the preceding year. This increase was attributed to generally favorable growing conditions, but also to an increase in innovation and the use of technology. New export markets such as Mexico and Cuba are providing incentives for greater production.

Logging has not yet caused widespread deforestation in Guyana, but there are concerns about the growing impact of Chinese and other foreign-based logging companies.

Other agricultural crops include coconuts, oranges, bananas, and plantains. Much of the land in the savannas is used for cattle ranching, since it is not fertile enough for agriculture.

FORESTRY AND FISHING   Tropical rain forest covers about three-quarters of Guyana, but until the 1990s it was underexploited, although there has always been some harvesting of trees, especially valuable hardwoods. In 1991, the government gave out the largest timber concession ever to a foreign company to produce plywood in a Georgetown factory. Plywood exports to the United States quadrupled as a result of this deal. Shrimp fishing in the ocean is the main focus of the commercial fishing industry. American and Japanese companies control much of this industry.

MINING   Bauxite, a metal used for producing aluminum, is an important resource. Bauxite mining began in Guyana in 1916, with the biggest mine in Linden and a second mine in the Berbice River region. Bauxite can be processed to produce calcium carbonate and alumina, which is the key component in aluminum. Although bauxite is a valuable export, it does not require large numbers of workers, since machines do much of the work. The commodity is also subject to large price fluctuations, which makes the exporting country vulnerable to economic ups and downs. In addition, more and more developed countries are now recycling aluminum, thereby reducing demand and pushing down prices. The global decline in bauxite demand prompted the Guyanese government to commission a top-to-bottom review of the industry in 2017 as it considers whether or not to have another alumina plant in the country.

A dredge ship mines gold from the bottoms of rivers and ponds.

Meanwhile, some in Guyana are saying "gold is the new bauxite." In fact, gold has become Guyana's leading export sector, bringing in nearly $1 billion in 2017. The country had been mining gold on a small-scale basis for many years, but only in 1993 did the government grant a large concession to a foreign firm. Since then, gold revenues have grown and made a significant contribution to export earnings. In 2018, Canadian gold-mining company Guyana Goldfields announced it would be building the Caribbean's first underground gold mines in Guyana, pending approval by the country's Environmental Protection Agency. Its existing gold mine in Aurora is an open-pit mine.

THE WORKFORCE

In 2017, Guyana estimated its labor force at about 547,928 people. However, not all of those potential workers were employed, with only about 54.5 percent actually working. That brought the total to about 295,881 people. Industry and commerce employed about 15.3 percent, agriculture employed 15.4 percent, and the service industry employed some 69.3 percent of the workers. The rest

A ferry carries passenger cars across the Essequibo River in Guyana.

of the population was either unemployed or engaged in activities not clearly defined.

TRADE

Guyana exports sugar, gold, bauxite, alumina, rice, shrimp, molasses, rum, and timber. Its main trading partners for exports in 2017 were Canada, the United States, Panama, the United Kingdom, Ukraine, Jamaica, and Trinidad and Tobago. Its chief imports are fuel and lubricants, heavy equipment, and manufactured consumer goods such as appliances. Guyana mainly imports from CARICOM countries, United States, China, and Suriname.

TRANSPORTATION

In the coastal zone, there are more than 367 miles (590 km) of paved and good-weather roads linking towns and villages. There are highways linking Linden and Georgetown that serve the mining and forestry sectors, and another links Linden with Lethem, on the Brazilian border. There are no public railways in the country, although two small private lines operate to transport minerals from the mines to the ports. Most people living in the interior of the country are either completely isolated from the coast or travel by air to make the journey over dense forests. Depending on the point of origin and the destination, river travel is also common, as there are some 3,666 miles (5,900 km) of navigable rivers. The Berbice, Demerara, and Essequibo Rivers are navigable by oceangoing vessels for 93 miles (150 km), 62 miles (100 km), and 49 miles (79 km), respectively.

Guyana had a government-owned airline called Guyana Airways Corporation, but it went bankrupt in 2001. A short-lived successor also failed. As of 2018, the country had no national air carrier. Passengers to and from Guyana are largely served by Caribbean Airlines, which flies out of Cheddi

Jagan International Airport at Timehri, 25 miles (40 km) south of Georgetown. Within Guyana, the regional carrier Roraima Airways serves travelers, tourists, and medical personnel out of Georgetown.

Guyana has two seaports. The older one is in Georgetown and was built to handle the transportation of sugar. The second is in New Amsterdam and was built primarily to ship bauxite and its derivatives. The three river ports are in Essequibo, Kaituma, and Linden.

INTERNET LINKS

http://agriculture.gov.gy
Guyana's Ministry of Agriculture site has up-to-date news and information.

https://www.cia.gov/library/PUBLICATIONS/the-world-factbook/geos/gy.html
The CIA World Factbook provides up-to-date statistics on Guyana's economy.

https://guysuco.gy/index.php/en
This is the site of the Guyana Sugar Corporation.

ENVIRONMENT

The jaguar (*Panthera onca*), the largest cat in the Americas, is the national animal of Guyana.

5

GUYANA IS A BEAUTIFUL LAND OF forests, rivers, waterfalls, and clean air. Human activities since colonial times have spoiled some of that beauty. The most affected areas are in the narrow coastal plain. Strips of swampy land were cleared to make way for agriculture and settlement. The huge hinterland remains largely unchanged except for forestry and mining activities in various locations.

Guyana traditionally does not face threats of volcanoes, hurricanes, or earthquakes. The main threat stems from flooding from sea-level rise. People coming from large urban cities are surprised at how spacious the urban centers in the plains are, even in the capital city of Georgetown. Wide avenues, gardens, and trees adjoin wooden buildings that are no higher than a few floors. Sea breezes from the Atlantic Ocean cool this tropical country. However, the charm is tarnished by Guyana's twin environmental problems—water pollution and waste disposal.

For Guyana the need to eradicate poverty without compromising its largely pristine natural environment can be a challenge. Still, Guyana's leaders and people look set to reverse the bad situations to make Guyana more attractive.

"There is an increasing awareness that climate change is not only an ecological and economic dilemma but also a social and psychological one. Guyana can expect prolonged dry spells, flash floods, and rising sea level." —Komalchand Dhiram, Guyana's Office for Climate Change

CAUSES AND EFFECTS OF POLLUTION

MINING IMPACTS   Guyana is rich in minerals. Gold, diamonds, bauxite, and granite are the targets of the mining sector. Kaolin, copper, lead, zinc, tungsten, nickel, iron, uranium, amethyst, green quartz, agate, jasper, and petroleum are also in demand. Small-scale miners pan for gold along rivers and creeks. Established miners dredge large sections of land or waterways.

Mining in Guyana attracts foreign investment, which in turn creates jobs for many Guyanese people. However, the methods of extraction have negative impacts on the natural environment. Rivers are filled with silt when hydraulic dredges are used to extract gold along the banks.

The use of chemicals in the extraction process is a major concern. For instance, caustic soda (sodium hydroxide) is used in bauxite production. To extract gold from hard rocks, mercury is used, with cyanide as a by-product. There have been reports of illness caused by the use of creek or river water in

Tainted wastewater from a gold mine flows into the forest.

In 2015, the ExxonMobil oil company drilled the Liza-1 well under the sea about 124 miles (200 km) off the Guyanese coastline. There it discovered a significant quantity of high-quality, oil-bearing sandstone reservoirs and quickly drilled more wells in the years that followed. The company reported that new discoveries contain estimated resources exceeding 4 billion barrels of oil equivalent, potentially producing 750,000 barrels per day by 2025.

This discovery could bring a huge economic boost to Guyana, which currently does not produce any oil. Some in Guyana—and beyond—are expecting untold riches to rain down upon the very poor country. According to its agreement with ExxonMobil, the Guyanese government stands to receive about half of the profits from the oil, after the company's initial costs are repaid. If so, within five years, Guyana could see its current gross domestic product of $3.6 billion triple.

However, the risks of it all going bad are quite high. As a small, poor country, Guyana has little experience with handling an economic project of such tremendous impact. The potential for misguided waste or worse, corruption, is no secret.

Environmentally, the oil company assures that the Liza project is expected to pose only minor risks. Guyana's EPA and many members of the public, however, are unconvinced and worry about potential oil spills. Nevertheless, the project is to proceed at full speed.

mining districts. Chemicals may have been carelessly released into the water, contaminating it.

Loss of villages and natural wildlife habitats is another issue associated with the mining sector. Soil erosion takes place when vegetation is cleared. This results in landslides during heavy storms.

LOGGING DEBRIS   Guyana's most precious asset is the rain forests; over 80 percent of Guyana is covered by rain forest. The forestry sector is necessary for Guyana's economic growth. However, the methods used for logging are sometimes not sustainable. Debris in the streams and rivers pollutes the water. Mangroves and the natural habitats of marine life are destroyed or threatened.

Logging activities also affect water channels through siltation of the water. Sediments from logging operations cloud the rivers.

Another potential hazard is sawmill waste. It raises biochemical oxygen demand, jeopardizing aquatic lives in the rivers. At the sawmills, rough sawn lumber is treated with chemicals to prevent attack from fungi and insects. Careless handling of chemicals can lead to poisoning of rivers and streams.

AGRICULTURAL POLLUTANTS   In a land of many rivers and springs, there is enough water for public use, agriculture, and industrial needs. Much of the water pollution on Guyana's coast is caused by the agricultural industry. The most prevalent agricultural pollutants are synthetic fertilizers that contain nitrate. In Guyana, rice is cultivated twice a year, of which about five months are spent using fertilizers to promote the growth of crops or pesticides to control bugs. Little consideration is given to runoff that hurts the ecosystem of both plants and fish.

Spillage is caused by careless handling of chemicals by laborers. Pesticides are used to control weeds in the coastal canals. They similarly impact the aquatic ecosystem as a whole.

CLIMATE CHANGE IMPACTS

Climate change is a problem that a small country like Guyana cannot solve by itself, but it will suffer the consequences regardless. A recent study concluded that by 2029, Guyana will annually see higher average temperatures than any previous year on record in the past 150 years. Meanwhile, on the planet's polar regions, the ice caps are melting at unprecedented rates, and sea levels are rising. For Guyana, this will soon become a crisis.

Sea-level rise on the Atlantic has already changed the nesting patterns of turtles on the beaches of Guyana. The beaches in Guyana have been the nesting place of turtles for many years. In recent times, locals have noticed changing nesting patterns. Turtles usually nest from March to August, but for the past few years the pattern has changed from mid-January to mid-July. Erosion of the beaches, which occurs naturally every thirty to thirty-five years, may be a contributing factor. Due to climate change, erosion is occurring before this cycle is up, and could happen within weeks.

Fish stock is already depleting from overharvesting. With climate change affecting sea levels and the temperature of the ocean, plankton, which generates the food chain for marine life, will be further reduced. Guyana's low-carbon development strategy includes giving fish stocks a chance to rebuild and sustain themselves.

DEFORESTATION

LOSS OF MANGROVE FORESTS   Guyana's forests remain in their pristine state today, but the swampy mangrove forests along the coast and Essequibo riverbanks had long been cleared by colonists to make way for the cultivation of crops. As a result, several species of mangrove and indigenous trees are extinct now. In their places, patches of paddy fields and sugarcane plantations are present.

What happens when the mangrove population decreases? The coast's natural defense against the Atlantic Ocean is lowered. The seawall prevents homes, sugarcane plantations, and rice fields from flooding each year. That wall cannot spare Guyana from the effects of climate change. Recently, severe flooding has hit Guyana almost every year, and it was particularly disastrous in 2005 and 2017. Since 90 percent of the population lives on this coast, which is already 3 feet (1 meter) below sea level, flooding is a particular danger to the country.

LOSS OF HARDWOODS   When it comes to forest harvesting, many locals believe their forests are inexhaustible. The often-heard boast "Dah wood kyan done, Man," meaning "the forest is inexhaustible," is common among loggers, both legal and illegal. Logging for timber can affect many species of hardwoods. Some of these species, such as the greenheart and purpleheart, are indigenous to Guyana. The current rate of harvesting for timber is unsustainable. It takes many decades to grow a canopy of trees, but these are felled in a matter of hours using an electric chainsaw.

NATIONAL PARKS AND RESERVES Traditionally, the indigenous Amerindians of Guyana have been the keepers of forestlands, and they have done an excellent job protecting the forests utilizing sustainable methods for their livelihood. With help from the government and rain forest conservation agencies, the Amerindians are able to reduce further damages to the forests and the ecosystem.

The Kaieteur National Park is one example of conservation. Located within one of the largest and most biodiverse rain forests in the world, the park covers 28,950 square miles (74,980 square km) of mountain range and lies between the Amazon and the Orinoco Rivers. Within Kaieteur are about twenty thousand different plant species, of which 35 percent are endemic, making it one of the three richest tropical wilderness areas on Earth. In addition, the park has a low human population density consisting mainly of Amerindian villages. Kaieteur is therefore one of the few places on Earth where all options for conservation are available.

It is a good thing that the government of Guyana is committed to keeping Guyana's forests standing. The low-carbon economic development strategy of 2009 targets an economic approach based on conservation and sustainable harvesting. It focuses on using the tropical forests to remove atmospheric carbon dioxide and slow the rate of climate change.

Another conservation effort is the Iwokrama Project. The Iwokrama International Center for Rainforest Conservation and Development (IIC)—a rain forest conservation charity—was established by Guyana and the Commonwealth. The IIC shows how tropical forests can be conserved and sustainably used for ecological, social, and economic benefits to local, national, and international communities.

WILDLIFE PROTECTION

Given Guyana's lush tropical forests, savannas, and low human population, the wildlife population should thrive. Still, more than thirty animals, such as the jaguar, leatherback turtle, harpy eagle, giant otter, caiman, and manatee, are on the Red List for endangered species of the International Union for

Conservation of Nature (IUCN). The Canje pheasant and the arapaima—the world's largest freshwater fish—are believed to be endangered too. Mining, logging, settlement, and hunting have all contributed to this sad fate.

Guyana and Conservation International set up the Konashen Community-Owned Conservation Area (COCA) to protect countless species of insects, arachnids, and other invertebrates. Many of these are still undiscovered and unnamed. The Konashen COCA provides a habitat for a remarkable diversity of amphibians, reptiles, birds, and mammals.

ECOTOURISM

Guyana has little to offer on its sixty-three beaches to match the facilities available on nearby Caribbean islands. But all that is changing—Guyana's ecotourism industry has taken off and is growing. Endangered sea turtles, various flora and fauna, rivers, and rain forests are preserved in their natural

A harpy eagle sits on a branch. The huge bird has a windspan of 8.2 feet (2.5 m).

state when tourists visit these sights. One can take a cruise down the Essequibo River in its natural rawness even as many of the world's rivers are being redistributed over agricultural lands or have dams built over them.

The Shell Beach Conservation Project serves as a haven to four of the eight endangered sea turtle species. The Botanical Gardens in Georgetown include 100 acres (40 ha) of plants and trees. The gardens are also home to endangered animals such as the manatee. Deeper in the forests, hundreds of birds such as the macaw, toucan, and harpy eagle can be spotted in their native habitats. Stranger animals and rarer ones can also be spotted. It is hoped that ecotourism will eventually replace mining and logging in economic value. Adventure tourism and nature tourism may not preserve the environment; ecotourism does it better.

WASTE TREATMENT

A major environmental issue for Guyana is waste management, including waste disposal, land use, and drainage. Urban centers such as Georgetown, New Amsterdam, Linden, Lethem, and Anna Regina have solid waste issues. Being centers for commerce, industry, administration, and residential use, they face similar problems of high population density, land use conflict, and poor infrastructure related to waste disposal.

To have a healthy environment, progressive communities employ a strategy to sort, recycle, convert, and dispose of their garbage and waste. In this respect, Guyana's solid waste management is far from adequate. Because Guyana's economy is concentrated in the narrow fertile coastal strip, towns and cities mushroomed to cater to the demands of the various industries. People here consume more processed food and packaged goods. Most waste in the past was biodegradable. The lack of resources and proper guidelines result in illegal garbage dumping, particularly of car tires and lumber yard waste. There is no proper landfill for final disposal of solid waste. The practice is to burn or dispose of waste in open-air dumping sites.

Another waste issue is sanitation. Without proper access to toilet facilities, people are at risk for poor health. In 2015, about 84 percent of the Guyanese population had access to improved sanitation facilities. More people in the rural areas are without these facilities.

In a time frame of only a few decades, human consumption patterns have drastically changed the environment. People have increased their use of energy, raw materials, and land. They have also produced more waste and destroyed some ecosystems. In terms of preserving its rain forests and ecosystems, Guyana has done better than many rain forest countries. Guyana is party to several environmental agreements on biodiversity, climate change, desertification, endangered species, ozone-layer protection, and law of the sea.

It will take much courage and determination to resolve the current environmental issues that are faced by this country. Guyana's environment has not reached critical levels that warrant quick action. The nation's approach is one of prevention rather than response.

INTERNET LINKS

https://climatechange.gov.gy/en
This is the site of Guyana's Office of Climate Change.

https://corporate.exxonmobil.com/en/company/worldwide -operations/locations/guyana/about-us/project-overview
The ExxonMobil site provides a detailed overview of the Liza project.

http://www.epaguyana.org/epa/
Read about the Environmental Protection Agency of Guyana here.

https://guyanatimesgy.com/guyana-to-take-on-eco-friendly-waste -disposal-system
This news article reflects the kinds of actions Guyana is taking to implement more environmentally sound waste disposal systems.

https://www.nytimes.com/2018/07/20/business/energy -environment/the-20-billion-question-for-guyana.html
This news article takes a hard look at the coming oil boom in Guyana.

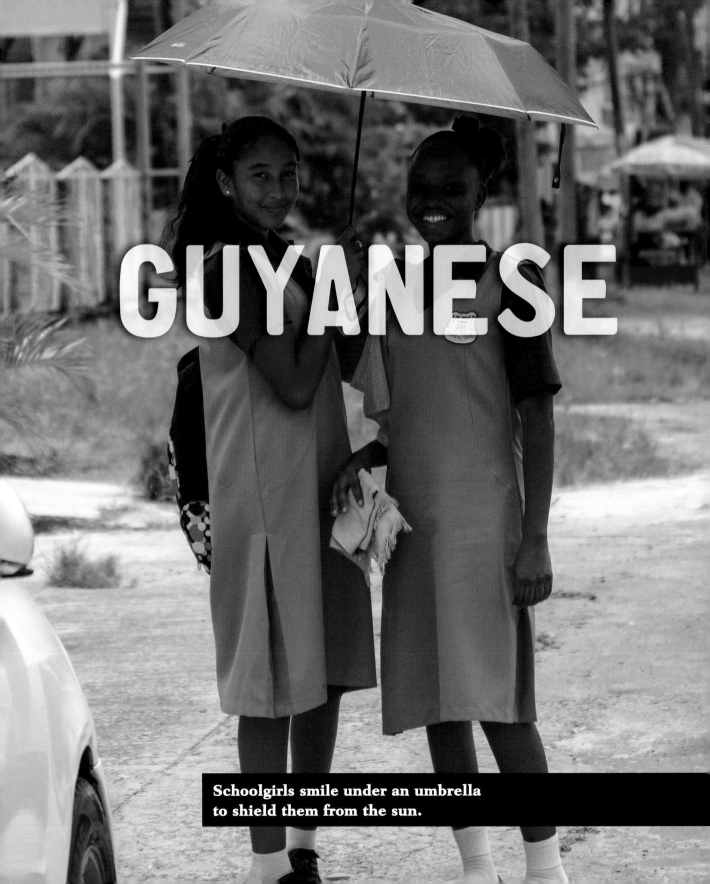

GUYANESE

Schoolgirls smile under an umbrella
to shield them from the sun.

6

ONE OF THE MANY NAMES FOR Guyana is the "Land of Six Peoples." This refers to the main ethnic groups that formed the majority of the country's population during the colonial era—East Indian, African, Amerindian, Chinese, European (largely British), and the Portuguese, who were regarded as a separate group because they came as indentured laborers. All but one of these groups—the exception being the Amerindians—came to, or were brought to, Guyana because of sugar.

Because of that history, today's Guyanese are a very diverse people. In 2018, the population was about 740,685, with East Indian and African-descended people making up more than two-thirds of the population. Different groups have come to occupy different niches in society as a result of the specific history of their arrival.

The national motto of Guyana is "One People, One Nation, One Destiny."

ETHNIC GROUPS

Although the popular conception of Guyana is that it's composed of six groups, the actual breakdown of the population is more complex, with a seventh important group—those of mixed African and European ancestry—included. Breakdown of the population by ethnicity cannot be precise in part because people sometimes identify themselves differently at different times and because census categories have changed over time. On the basis of the most recent estimates and figures available, the following percentages can be identified:

- Indo-Guyanese (people descended from East Indian immigrants): 39.8 percent
- Afro-Guyanese (people descended from enslaved Africans): 29.3 percent
- Mixed (primarily people of African and European ancestry): 19.9 percent
- Amerindians (indigenous groups): 10.5 percent
- Others (including Chinese, Portuguese, and other Europeans): 0.5 percent

Guyanese of all backgrounds shop at the popular Stabroek Market in Georgetown.

The percentages above make clear that the two largest groups are those of East Indian and African descent. The mixed group includes people with both African and European ancestors. Under slavery, it was not uncommon for a white master to have children with his female slaves. Later, when indentured laborers arrived without wives of their own, they sometimes married women of African origin.

Portuguese and Chinese are also included in the "six" races, although their numbers are quite small. Whites, or those of European descent, are also a tiny minority. Amerindians represent a larger percentage of the population. Guyana is one of the few countries in the Americas where the number of original people has held steady or even increased in the twenty-first century.

Not only is the population as a whole complexly divided by ethnicity, but even within these larger categories there are differences and specificities.

INDO-GUYANESE People of East Indian descent make up the largest ethnic group. They can be divided into two subgroups—those who practice Hinduism and those who practice Islam as their religion. Unlike in India, where these differences have led to war and the separation of Pakistan and Bangladesh from India, the two subgroups of Indo-Guyanese live amicably in Guyana.

AFRO-GUYANESE The Afro-Guyanese tend to live in towns, especially Georgetown. When enslaved people were finally freed in the nineteenth century, they quickly chose to distance themselves from plantation society. Many moved to urban areas and educated themselves to occupy better-paying positions. From there, they expanded into the civil service and the bauxite industry. Today, the Afro-Guyanese make up about 50 percent of the urban population.

The descendants of African slaves and the mixture of these people with Europeans make up what is called Creole society. Although the slaves came from many different cultural groups in West Africa, they have lost most of the cultural and linguistic characteristics that separated them. This is a very common process wherever enslaved peoples were brought to live and is the result of the conditions of slavery in which the slaves were not allowed to maintain cultural differences among themselves. The main differences among the Afro-Guyanese are those of color, with the mixed group traditionally occupying a slightly higher position in society.

AMERINDIANS   The Amerindian group is not uniform but is made up of people from a number of smaller linguistic and cultural groups. Three indigenous languages are represented among Guyana's Amerindians—Carib, Arawak, and Warao (also spelled Warrau).

Among the Carib-speaking groups found in modern Guyana are the Akawáio; Patamuno (a subtribe of the Akawáio); Arekuna; Parukoto and Taulipáng (both subgroups of the Arekuna); Ingarikó; and Makushí.

The Akawáio live near the Guyana-Venezuela-Brazil border. About 25 percent continue to practice traditional ways, whereas the rest have been converted to Christianity. The Patamuno live in the Pakaraima Mountains between the Ireng River and the Kaieteur escarpment. They have mostly integrated into the Guyanese cash economy.

The Arekuna arrived in Guyana in the 1920s when Seventh-Day Adventist missionaries were expelled from Venezuela. They followed the missionaries and still live in the Paruima area of Guyana. The Parukoto live on both sides of the border with Venezuela and experienced population growth in the twentieth century due to missionary work and the introduction of Western medicine. The Taulipáng live near Roraima. This group was almost decimated by the mass immigration of Brazilians into their territory in the mid-nineteenth century. They are still aware of their tribal heritage, but more and more of them speak Portuguese and Spanish as their first languages.

The Makushí live in the savanna region of Rupununi and in the southern Pakaraimas of Guyana and Venezuela. They are a large group who have adapted to Guyanese values and technology. The majority practice animism, although some have adopted Christianity. In Rupununi, many are cattle ranchers.

The Ingarikó live near the Guyana-Brazil border on the Mau River. They have had some contact with Brazilian society, but they have also managed to maintain their traditional language and culture. They are well known for basket weaving using liana, titica, and aruma fibers. Their beautiful handicrafts are in high demand.

The second group are the Warao, who live in the lowland delta of the Orinoco River in northeastern Venezuela and western Guyana. Unlike forest dwellers, these people are mostly dependent on fishing and are proficient boatbuilders.

The third group of indigenous people are the Arawalk speakers, the Locono and Taruma.

The Locono live along the coast from the Moruka River in Guyana to the Brazil—French Guiana border. Their population is growing, and they have integrated into the coastal economy of the region.

The story of the Taruma is tragic. They migrated into the southern part of Guyana in the eighteenth century and were about five hundred strong in the nineteenth century. In the 1920s, an epidemic of influenza almost wiped out the Taruma. Today there are a few descendants of this group who still refer to themselves as Taruma.

Unfortunately, stories like that of the Taruma are common because indigenous people with no natural immunity to many European diseases fell sick when Europeans arrived. These diseases were introduced to the Amazon by miners and explorers and spread very rapidly. It is therefore remarkable that Guyana's population of indigenous people rose by 22,097 between 1991 and 2002. This represents an annual growth of 3.5 percent.

PORTUGUESE Most of the Portuguese indentured laborers came from a single island off the coast of Portugal—Madeira. This is one of the islands of the Azores group. Due to poverty and a tradition of immigration, Madeira has supplied many labor needs around the world from the nineteenth century to the present.

CHINESE For the most part, Chinese workers came from the south of China, and therefore they spoke Cantonese rather than the northern and dominant Chinese language, Mandarin. Much like Madeira, the region of Canton, which is now called Guangdong, has traditionally been poorer than the north and was a major exporter of workers to many parts of the world throughout the nineteenth and early twentieth centuries.

Most people live in the flat coastal regions, as seen in this aerial view of the Georgetown region.

POPULATION PATTERNS

Guyana has an unusual demographic pattern. On the one hand, because 90 percent of the people live in a small area along the coast, Guyana appears to be overpopulated and experiences the problems that accompany that condition—urban crime and inadequate public services. On the other hand, given the actual size of the country, the average population density is only about 8.5 people per square mile (3.5 people per sq km). That means Guyana is underpopulated and experiences problems associated with having too few people, such as a failure to fully exploit its natural resources because of the lack of labor.

Growth-wise, Guyana experienced a fairly constant growth pattern throughout most of the twentieth century. The population reached a peak of more than one million in the late 1980s. A significant factor in this growth was the introduction of DDT in the 1940s to kill mosquitoes and combat malaria.

LAURENS STORM VAN GRAVESANDE *This man was the Dutch governor of the colony of Essequibo from 1742 to 1752. In 1746, he opened up the Demerara region for colonization and encouraged many Dutch and British planters to move from their estates in the Caribbean islands. He is remembered for his work as governor and also for his support for humane treatment of slaves on the plantations.*

CUFFY *In 1763, one of the most successful slave rebellions of the eighteenth century took place in Berbice colony, then under Dutch control. The rebellion started in February that year on the Magdalenenburg plantation and quickly spread to other plantations in the area. By the end of March, almost the whole colony was under slave control, and their leaders swore that they would never return to a life of servility and cruelty. One of these slave leaders was Cuffy. He and the other slaves managed to hold the colony for ten months despite Dutch efforts to reclaim it. With the help of Amerindians and soldiers from the Netherlands, the colony was finally retaken by the end of the year, and the rebel leaders were rounded up and executed. Cuffy is regarded as a hero in Guyana for his part in this rebellion, and there is a statue of him in Georgetown.*

REVEREND JOHN SMITH *A member of the London Missionary Society, Smith came to work in Guyana in the early nineteenth century. He campaigned against the atrocities committed by the planters against their slaves. After a slave uprising in Demerara colony in 1823, he was falsely accused of having helped the slaves to rebel. He was imprisoned and died in prison. His death added fuel to the abolitionist movement—the movement to end slavery—in Britain.*

WALTER RODNEY *was an acclaimed historian who wrote about European exploitation and imperialism in the Caribbean and Guyana; his most important work was* How Europe Underdeveloped Africa, *published in 1972. He was also a founding member of the Working People's Alliance, a social democratic political party, and this earned him the animosity of the dictatorial government of Forbes Burnham.*

Rodney was assassinated in 1980 at the age of thirty-eight. Government forces were widely believed to have been involved in his murder. Despite a government directive that no civil servants should attend his funeral, thousands of people accompanied his body on the day of the funeral. He became a symbol of the oppression of the Burnham government.

ETHNIC TENSIONS

The main ethnic tension exists between the two largest groups, the Indo-Guyanese and Afro-Guyanese. The Afro-Guyanese are generally considered by others—and consider themselves—almost native to the country, whereas the Indo-Guyanese are usually grouped with the Portuguese and the Chinese as "immigrants." These two groups have competed since independence for dominance in politics, with the PPP representing people of East Indian descent and the PNC being largely supported by the Afro-Guyanese.

This ethnic tension is perhaps not surprising given the history of relations between the two groups under colonialism. The British used ethnic and racial differences to prevent groups of workers from uniting against the exploitative planter class. Under extreme economic pressure, ethnic tensions can escalate.

GUYANESE DIASPORA

Guyana's emigration rate is among the highest in the world—more than 55 percent of its citizens reside abroad. The largest overseas communities

Guyanese students at Lesley University in Massachusetts graduate from a bachelor's counseling program geared specifically toward helping Guyananese victims of abuse.

of Guyanese expatriates are in the United States (about 86,120), the United Kingdom (20,872), Canada (14,560), and the Netherlands (328). Many of these people are working abroad and sending money home in the form of remittances.

Guyana, therefore, is one of the largest recipients of remittances relative to GDP among Latin American and Caribbean countries. These monies from family members working abroad are often a vital source of income for many Guyanese, but there is a down side to the situation as well. The ongoing emigration of large numbers of skilled workers deprives Guyana of professionals in health care and other key sectors. More than 80 percent of Guyanese nationals with university- and professional-level educations have emigrated, causing a brain drain at home. This loss naturally impacts Guyana's economy in a negative way.

The number of people Guyana has lost to other countries is even higher when the descendents of earlier emigrants are included. Shirley Chisholm (1924—2005), who became the first black woman elected to the US Congress in 1968, traced her Guyanese roots to her father, an early emigrant from British Guiana. More recently, pop star Rihanna's mother is a Guyanese émigré. Many people left Guyana during the uncertain time of the Forbes Burnham government, but the outward tide continues to the present as people seek better opportunities abroad.

INTERNET LINKS

https://libcom.org/library/street-speech-walter-rodney
This transcript of a street speech given by Walter Rodney in the 1970s addresses racial tensions in Guyana.

http://worldpopulationreview.com/countries/guyana-population
This sites provides statistics relating to Guyana's demographics.

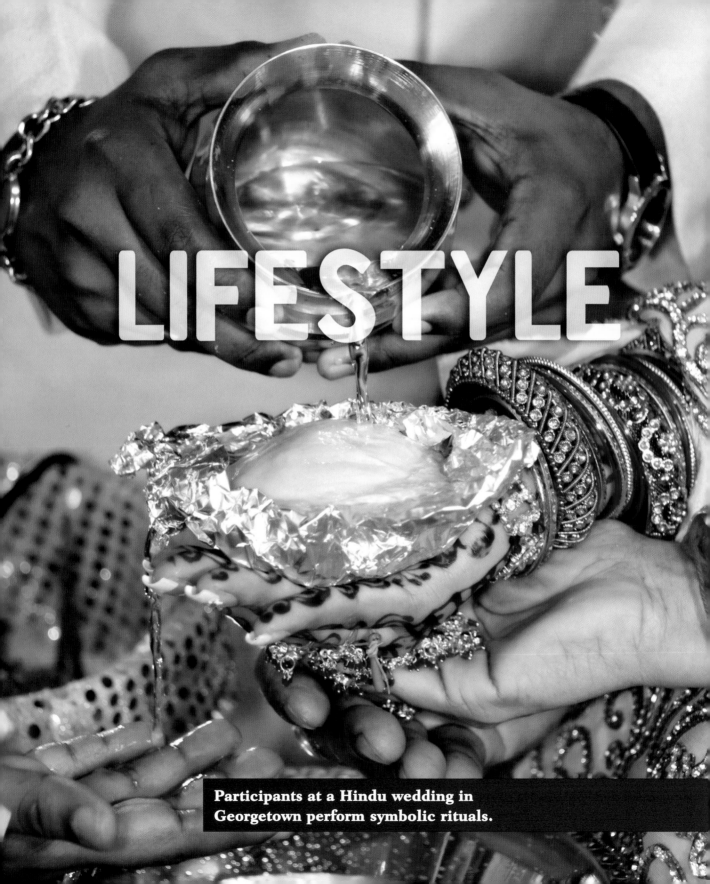

LIFESTYLE

Participants at a Hindu wedding in Georgetown perform symbolic rituals.

7

W ITH SUCH A DIVERSE ETHNIC MIX, it is impossible to generalize about the Guyanese people and their lifestyle. The most important differences are those between rural and urban dwellers and between Indo- and Afro-Guyanese cultures. Some social institutions are shared by all the Guyanese, such as education and health, but even in these areas, there are some differences.

MARRIAGE AND FAMILY STRUCTURE

There are three main patterns of family life in Guyana, and they correspond roughly to ethnic and class groupings. Due to different conditions of life under the colonial system, the Afro-, Indo-, and Euro-Guyanese developed different types of family structures or modified those that they brought with them from their country of origin.

AFRO-GUYANESE   As slaves, Africans were not allowed to maintain their original kinship and family ties, and much of the African culture they came with died out quickly on the plantations. In its place, European models were enforced. The Afro-Guyanese created what became known

Among the Hindu and Muslim Guyanese, arranged marriages are less common than they once were, but do still occur, often early in life. Middle-class and professional people tend to have more options and marry a bit later.

Among the Afro-Guyanese, formal marriage is less common, and more households are headed by women.

as Creole culture, the result of copying European models with modifications brought about by poverty.

Today Afro-Guyanese family structure has two facets—the reality and the ideal. In the ideal family, young people marry at a formal wedding and then set up house together where the man works and his wife stays at home. The reality for the majority of Creoles or Afro-Guyanese is radically different, however. Because men have not been able to guarantee financial support for their families, many women have chosen not to marry and instead raise their children (often by different men) in the homes where the women were born, with their mothers, grandmothers, and sisters to help. Women become the main support of the family, and the men move in and out of this unit, depending on whether they are able to provide some support. This matrifocal, or mother-centered, pattern is common across the Caribbean.

INDO-GUYANESE Both the ideal and reality are also quite different among the Guyanese of East Indian descent. As indentured laborers, East Indians were encouraged to maintain their culture and not mix with either the former slaves or other indentured groups. At the end of their contract, they were encouraged to stay in the colony with grants of small plots of land near the sugarcane estates. This kept them available for paid work on the plantations and avoided payment of their passage home—which was part of the indenture contract. As more and more East Indians settled in the rural areas, they brought their wives over and tried to re-create their traditional family structure. They managed to keep some of their traditions alive, but some were not sustainable because there were too few of their people.

One cultural trait that was not maintained was the caste system, which in this case was just as well. Traditionally, India observed—and still does, in some places—a rigid social hierarchy. People are considered more or less religiously pure, according to the traditional job held by members of the family. All families doing the same work are considered part of the same caste. In India, people generally do not marry outside of their caste, and the rules are very strict, especially in rural areas.

In Guyana, East Indians could not continue this custom because there were not enough people from each caste to provide a suitable range of marriageable partners. Nevertheless, other features of Indian social life were maintained, including religion and a strong family life. Today, the Indo-Guyanese place a great deal of emphasis on marriage, children, and maintaining ties with the extended family. Marriages are no longer necessarily arranged by the parents. Some young people assert their right to choose their own partners. However, both sets of parents do get involved in preparing for the wedding and helping the young couple get started in life.

Since the Indo-Guyanese can be either Muslim or Hindu, they used to marry only within their religion. That is still the ideal and the norm, but marriages across religious lines are possible, if not encouraged. What is not usually allowed by families is marriage into other ethnic groups, particularly Creole society. In this way, culture has been preserved from one generation to the next. Hindu weddings are common colorful events on the weekends in rural areas during the dry season.

EURO-GUYANESE   The third cultural pattern is the one set by European immigrants. In Guyana, as in other colonies, the Europeans were the wealthiest and could afford elaborate weddings and stable marriages. Their ideal was to marry only people of high rank and white ethnic background. Family ties are important because this group is so small today that they must rely on one another for help.

RURAL VERSUS URBAN LIVING

Most of the Indo-Guyanese live in small rural villages along the coast. Here traditional rites and festivities are maintained more strictly, and family ties are broadened with each generation's marriages. A marriage here means not just the union of two young people but also of their families. This is the basis for social cohesion.

After the prospective bride and groom have convinced their parents to accept their choice of partner, the young people step aside and the older generation takes over. There are many steps that have to be followed for the wedding to conform to the rules of the Hindu religion and the local traditions of the family or village. Some of the events that make up a wedding in Guyana include:

- **Chekai** *(che-KAI), or the engagement ceremony. The bride's father offers gifts to the groom's father, and a religious scholar known as a pandit invokes the blessings of Hindu gods and goddesses. Other male members of the community are present to show that they approve of the marriage.*
- **Mati-kore** *(MAH-tee KOR-ay), or "Digging the Dirt." This is performed a couple of nights before the wedding at both the bride's and groom's houses. The women of the family, including the mothers of the bride and groom and their aunts, meet at each other's houses to sing Hindi songs and play traditional instruments. On the way home, they pick up dirt and carry it into their houses. Both groups of women also plant a green bamboo pole, called a nuptial pole, in each of their courtyards. The bamboo signifies the continuity of the family. In the bride's house, the* marua *(mah-ROO-ah), or the booth where the wedding will be performed, is built on this night, and a pandit lights a sacred fire there.*
- **Tilak** *(TEE-lahk). This is another ceremony that takes place at the groom's house. The pandit will ask the groom to behave himself and dedicate his life to his bride.*
- **Hardi** *(HAHR-dee). The bride and groom are purified by pandits, and neighbors bring small gifts to each house.*
- **Kumari-patra** *(koo-MAHR-ee PAH-trah) and* **kumar-patra** *(koo-MAHR PAH-trah). These ceremonies are held to mark the end of childhood for both bride and groom.*
- **Baryat** *(bar-YAHT). The groom arrives at the house of the bride. He wears a Western suit with a traditional covering, called a* jama *(JAH-mah), and a special headdress called a pat-mauri (PAT-MOW-ree).*
- **Milap** *(MEE-lahp). The baryat is received 15 to 20 yards (14 to 18 m) from the bride's house. The bride's father pays the groom's father a sum of money.*

- **Janwas** (*JAHN-wahs*). *The groom's party is formally welcomed.*
- **Dwar pooja** (*DWAR POO-jah*). *A ceremony is performed at the door of the bride's house that welcomes the groom and asks for the blessings of all the gods.*
- **Parchay** (*PAHR-chee*). *The bride's mother welcomes the groom inside the house.*
- **Naichu** (*NAI-choo*). *A gift-giving ceremony when everyone present offers gifts to the bride seated under the nuptial pole. She is usually dressed in a beautiful traditional Indian dress called a sari, a long piece of fine fabric wrapped around her waist and thrown over one shoulder. Under that she wears a choli, or a tight-fitting, short-sleeved T-shirt, and lots of gold jewelry.*
- **Vivah** (*VEE-vah*). *The older brother of the groom promises to take care of the bride and she is told to respect him as her older brother.*
- **Kanya dan** (*KAHN-yah DAHN*). *This ceremony is to "give the maiden away." It takes place under the marua. The bride sits beside her father, and he places her hand into the hand of the groom, who accepts it. Then the bride moves to sit beside her new husband.*
- **Lava havan** (*LAH-vah HAH-vahn*). Lava (*fried rice*) *is burned in the* havan, *or fire pit, under the nuptial pole. The bride and groom throw rice into the fire while the pandit recites sacred texts.*
- **Bhanwar** (*BAHN-wahr*). *The bride and groom walk around the pole seven times, with the bride in the lead for four circuits and the groom leading for three. This creates a sacred tie between them, with Agni, the fire god, as witness.*
- **Sat bachan** (*SAHT BAH-chahn*). *The groom vows to look after the bride and consult her in all important family matters. Then he puts* sendoor (*SEN-door*), *a special paste, on the part in her hair and gives her a ring. This completes the ceremony.*

Sometimes, at this point, the bride leaves to change into a formal white Western wedding dress and goes away with the groom to begin their married life. Not only does a Hindu wedding involve many steps and rituals, but it is also highly religious, with a pandit presiding over nearly every phase. It involves members of both families and the wider community.

A thatched-roof house is a typical abode in Guyana's rural regions.

In urban centers, marriage is still important and still involves the two families, but may not be as significant in terms of economic cooperation and the inheritance of land and other forms of wealth. Creole people live in both cities and villages, but are more urban than rural. In general urban families are smaller due to the constraints of housing. At the same time there are more families that include the father, since men are more likely to find work and be able to live near both their families and their jobs.

Rural families are often poorer but live in better conditions than the poor of the cities, who must contend with unsanitary conditions and higher crime rates. In the countryside, because people know one another, it is not as easy to get away with crimes against your neighbors. The benefits of city living include easier access to education and other services and greater potential for paid employment for those who do not have land in the countryside.

HOUSING

Housing styles reflect wealth and local conditions. Traditional building patterns on the coast have left a heritage of beautiful, raised wooden houses in cities such as Georgetown. Farther inland, houses take on different shapes depending on their location, from the more ranch-like designs in the savanna to conical, thatched Amerindian houses in the more isolated settlements. The rural poor may not have electricity and will rely on kerosene, gas, and oil lamps for lighting. For cooking, they use kerosene, wood, and coal.

Formal dress for men in Guyana used to require a long-sleeved cuffed shirt and trousers. In the intense heat and humidity of the tropics, this was not a comfortable option. Since independence, political leaders have been popularizing a type of shirt called a shirt-jac. (In Spanish-speaking Caribbean countries, it's called a guayabera.*) This is buttoned up but not tucked in and has at least three pockets on the front. It is white or some other light color and made of light fabrics such as cotton. The pockets can be decorated with pleats, but otherwise the shirt is unadorned. It is also open in a "V" at the top, with lapels. As a more practical formal dress, the shirt-jac has become quite popular with Guyanese men.*

EDUCATION AND LITERACY

Guyanese children are given free education from the age of three to early adulthood. Elementary education covers the first six years, while secondary education begins at twelve years of age and lasts for five to seven years, divided into two cycles of five and two years. In 2015, Guyana's literacy rate was 88.5 percent for people over the age of fifteen.

The Australian cricket player Alyssa Healy poses with local children during a Schools and Community Outreach Program event at East Reimveldt Secondary School in Georgetown in 2018.

Schools had already been suffering from severe underfunding, as well as staffing and supply problems, after Forbes Burnham made them public in 1976. During the economic crisis of the 1980s, however, the quality of education declined tremendously. Student scores plummeted further in the 1990s. There are several reasons for this deterioration.

The main problem is that the government did not have the money to fund a completely free system. School buildings were not properly maintained, and there were shortages of textbooks and teaching materials. Under the PNC dictatorship, schools were also used to promote party politics and loyalty. Teachers who did not agree were fired, leaving fewer qualified teachers and an atmosphere of insecurity in the teaching profession. Since the ERP was

"Pork-knockers" is the common term for men who spend their lives in Guyana's interior, sifting through river mud looking for rough diamonds and gold nuggets. Pork-knockers used to be mostly Afro-Guyanese, but in recent years, young Indo-Guyanese are trying their hand, too.

The gold miners use pumps to dredge the silt from the bottom of the river into pans with mesh at the bottom. The silt is then separated from larger pebbles and rocks, some of which contain gold. The miners then melt the gold nuggets together and, when they have enough, make their way into the nearest settlement to sell their hard-earned riches.

Diamond hunters dig holes along the riverbanks and sort through the mud and rocks looking for gems. Although Guyana's diamonds are small in size, they are of high quality. The largest diamond ever found, in 1970, was eight carats, but it mysteriously disappeared. The three men who found that diamond are still pork-knockers and are as poor as ever. Although the pork-knockers are constantly finding gold and diamonds, they never get rich because when they sell their treasures, they spend all their money immediately, eating, drinking, and living well after spending weeks in the jungle. This is much the same pattern as what happened during the nineteenth-century gold rush in the United States.

implemented to repair the economy, Guyana lost many of its professionals, including teachers, to emigration. All of these factors helped create a poor learning environment. The situation has improved somewhat thanks to external funding and an increased education budget from the government in the 2000s.

In 2016, Guyana allocated $40.3 billion of its budget, or 17.5 percent of its GDP, to education, a huge leap from the 3.8 percent of GDP spent from 2006 to 2012. This is proportionately a very high percentage, as compared to other nations, and reflects the government's view that education is the key to raising the country's overall social and economic position.

Students in Guyana undergo a four- to seven-year program to prepare for the basic Caribbean Examination Council (CXC) examination or the London General Certificate of Education (GCE), Advanced Level. Beyond secondary school, there are several technical and vocational institutes and two teacher-training colleges, as well as a national university. The University of Guyana was set up after independence. It is free to Guyanese citizens and offers undergraduate degrees in the arts and sciences and a master's degree in history.

HEALTH

In 2018, Guyana's average life expectancy at birth was 68.9 years, with males averaging 65.9 years and females 72.1 years. These statistics mean that a child born in 2018—assuming conditions in Guyana stay the same—could look forward to living that many years, on average, depending on gender. Life expectancy is an important measure that indicates a country's overall general health and well-being. These statistics are often used to compare one country to another, and also to evaluate a country's progress, or lack of it, in the realms of health and safety. Guyana's life expectancy figures are relatively low, ranking it at 164 out of 223 countries. For comparison, the United States ranked 45 with an average of 80 years. Japan topped the list (not counting tiny Monaco) with 85.5, and Afghanistan ranked lowest, with 52.1.

Other statistics that indicate a country's general health include the infant mortality rate and the maternal mortality rate. In these, as well, Guyana does fairly poorly, among the worst—or the worst—in South America.

Disturbingly, a 2014 report by the World Health Organization (WHO) cited Guyana as the country with the highest suicide rate in the world—44.2 suicides per 100,000 deaths, four times the global average. By 2017, however, the rate had dropped 32 percent, to 30.2 suicides per 100,000 deaths (46.6 male. 14.2 female), taking Guyana out of the dreadful top spot in this category. Nevertheless, it still had the third-highest suicide rate in the world, surpassed by Russia and Lithuania.

No one factor can explain Guyana's high incidence of suicide, but some of the factors contributing to the risk include poverty, a pervasive stigma about mental illness, access to lethal chemicals, alcohol misuse, interpersonal violence, family dysfunction, and insufficient mental health resources.

TROPICAL DISEASES   As a tropical country, Guyana is vulnerable to many of the world's most infectious and deadly diseases. Dengue fever is on the rise, and typhoid is also dominant all around Guyana. Gastroenteritis, a disease

KALI MAI: DESTRUCTION OF EVIL FORCES

There is a small group of people who believe in the powers of a specific ritual to cure sick people, particularly those with emotional and psychological problems. The ritual is called Kali Mai Puja. Puja is an East Indian word for a religious ritual that shows devotion to one of the Hindu gods or goddesses. In this particular ritual, people pray to the goddess Kali for help. Kali is believed to be the goddess of destruction, but she can also destroy evil. A Kali Mai Puja requires a specialist called a pujari *(POO-jah-ree) to preside over the activities.*

This person can be of either gender and can come from any cultural background. Followers of Kali Mai say that the rituals are drawn from all the religions in Guyana and therefore can work for anyone. Kali Mai works through possession by spirits and animal sacrifice. There is even a Kali Mai Church, and the only requirement for membership is for a person to reject his or her former religious beliefs. Some psychologists have used Kali Mai pujaris to help with their patients' problems. Although not widely popular, this is a distinctly Guyanese religion and an alternative healing practice.

of the stomach and intestines, is common, as are intestinal parasites. One intestinal parasite prevalent in Guyana is microfilaria, which, if it is not treated, causes noninfectious elephantiasis, the extreme growth of parts of the body to the point where they cannot be structurally supported.

Malaria is no longer a problem along the coast, but it is still very common in inland areas above 2,953 feet (900 m). Malaria is passed on by the anopheles mosquito when it bites humans. Certain kinds of malaria are fatal. Yellow fever is also present, and many types of skin fungal infections are endemic due to the high humidity and lack of medical treatment. Tuberculosis has plagued Guyana for a long time, and the government has sponsored several anti-tuberculosis campaigns. This disease is highly contagious and difficult to control. There are also occasional hepatitis epidemics in populated areas.

Many of these diseases, especially in coastal areas, result from inadequate supplies of water and inadequate public hygiene. Most rainwater and used water is collected in open drains in the cities and towns. In richer neighborhoods, sewage is disposed of through septic tanks, but in the poorer areas, it is allowed to run off in open drains. Similarly, garbage is allowed to pile up in public places in poorer areas. Stagnant water and garbage encourage the spread of diseases such as typhoid, dengue, gastroenteritis, and parasitic infections. Public water supplies are also unsafe in both rural and urban areas.

Some Guyanese turn to an alternative healing practice called Kali Mai Puja (KAH-lee MAI POO-jah). Kali Mai, also known as Mother Kali, is a goddess of South Asian origin that is presently worshipped in numerous churches. Healing rituals and services are an integral part of Kali worship, which attracts many devotees because of their desire to alleviate any number of problems. Worship of Kali occurs every Sunday at various churches or *mandirs*, where a *puja* is performed for all the deities housed in the mandir and is then followed by a number of different healing services.

INTERNET LINKS

https://www.education.gov.gy
This is the site of the Guyana Ministry of Education.

https://www.guyanatimesinternational.com/?p=46358
The *Guyana Times* discusses the various wedding traditions in the country.

https://www.npr.org/sections/goatsandsoda/2018/06/29/ 622615518/trying-to-stop-suicide-guyana-aims-to-bring-down -its-high-rate
This story takes a close look at the difficult topic of suicide in Guyana.

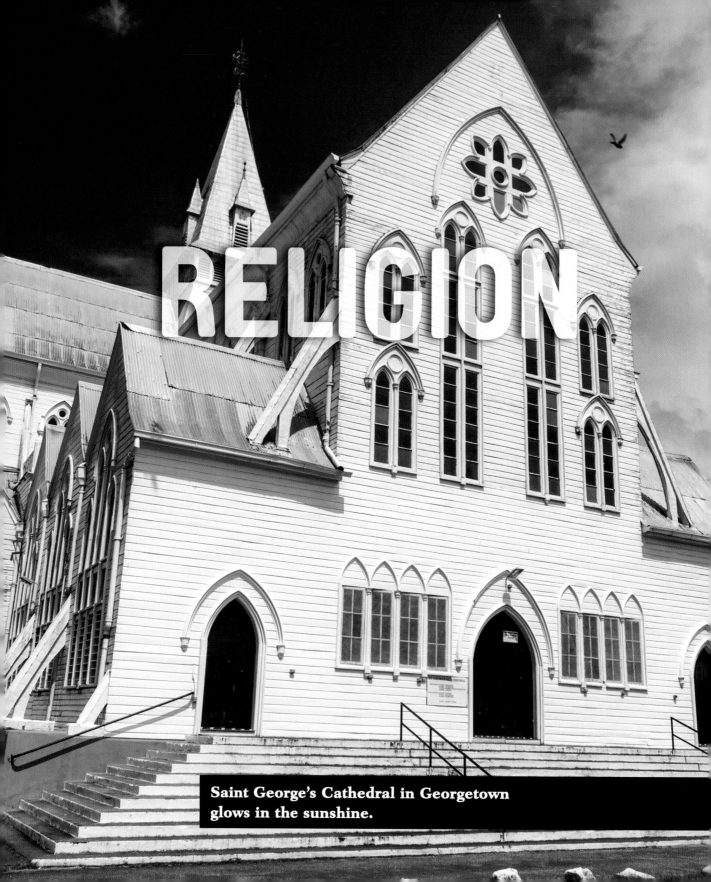

RELIGION

Saint George's Cathedral in Georgetown
glows in the sunshine.

A S WITH ETHNICITY, DIVERSITY IS the key to religion in Guyana. Almost all of the world's main religions have some representation in the nation, along with minor cults and folk belief systems. Religion has played an important role in historical and modern-day political relations among the various groups.

THE MAIN FORMAL RELIGIONS

According to statistics from 2012, 62 percent of Guyanese were Christian, and most of them were Protestants, with Pentecostals making up 22.8 percent of the population. Hindus, mainly of East Indian descent, represented 24.8 percent; Muslims made up 7.1 percent. Most Muslims in Guyana are East Indian, but there are a few Afro-Guyanese Muslims as well.

CHRISTIANS The Anglican Church is the official church of England. The religion was brought to Guyana by British planters during the colonial period. It was the state religion of British Guiana until independence in 1966. The Anglican Church is similar to the Roman Catholic Church in many ways, but Anglicans do not regard the Pope as the head of the church. The English monarch has the constitutional title of Supreme Governor of the Church of England. Most Creoles adopted this religion while they were

8

Saint George's Cathedral in Georgetown dates to 1894 and is a national monument. The Anglican church is said to be the world's tallest wooden church, at 143 feet (43.5 m), and is built largely from a native hardwood called greenheart.

The interior of Saint George's Cathedral in Georgetown reveals Gothic arches and flying buttresses, all made of wood.

slaves, and their descendants continue to practice it today. Since all education in Guyana was controlled by church groups until 1956, there was some pressure for East Indian children to convert while they attended school. Some did so, but most have held on to Hinduism and Islam, their religions of birth.

Protestants of many denominations are now present in Guyana, with the Anglican Church itself now only accounting for a tiny 5.2 percent of the total population. Roman Catholicism, on the other hand, is practiced by a small 7.1 percent of the Guyanese people.

HINDUS   Hinduism is the dominant religion in India. It is a pantheistic religion, which means that there are many different deities, or gods. There are three major sects in Hinduism: Saivism, Vaishnavism, and Shaktism. Lord Siva is regarded as the chief deity in Saivism. Followers can be identified with a mark of three horizontal stripes across their foreheads. The East Indian immigrants

AWACAIPU AND THE COMING OF THE MILLENNIUM

Throughout the nineteenth century, European churches sent many missionaries to the Americas to try to convert indigenous people to Christianity. Often their influence was direct, in the form of missions established in the interior of countries such as Guyana. However, their teachings were sometimes indirectly powerful, as individuals carried their ideas back from trading posts or settlements.

One such incident took place when Awacaipu, a shaman of the Arekuna tribe, returned from living in Georgetown. He had been employed by Robert Schomburgk (1804–1865), a German scientist and traveler with the Royal Geographical Society. Awacaipu had learned English and was very impressed by the teachings of the European missionaries.

When he returned to his group, he told them of the coming of the millennium, which Amerindian shamans believed was a new age of material plenty. In Awacaipu's version, the millennium would bring the power of white people to Amerindians. However, those who would enjoy this advantage must first die within a stipulated three-day period. They would then come back to life with new white bodies and meet their families at the slopes of Mount Roraima. They would rule over other brown-skinned men who had not undergone this ordeal. A few hundred followers clubbed one another to death over the next three days. When the dead people failed to reappear after two weeks, the survivors turned on Awacaipu and killed him.

Millennial movements such as this have been common wherever colonialism reached indigenous people whose lifestyle was radically different from that of the Europeans. The result was often that the indigenous people believed that Europeans possessed magic and only through extreme practices such as suicide could they become like the Europeans.

to Guyana belonged to the Hindu sect of Vaishnavism. Adherents of this sect regard Lord Vishnu as the supreme creator. They can be identified with a U-shaped mark and a long stripe between the two arms of the U across their foreheads. Followers of Shaktism worship Devi or the Mother Goddess as the creator of all.

Since 1875, there have been two schools of Hinduism—Sanatan Dharam, or the Orthodox school, and Arya Samaj, or the Reformist school. Followers of

Sanatan Dharam believe in the most traditional of Hindu writings and practices. They worship all the traditional gods and goddesses, such as Ganesha, Lakshmi, and Agni, and believe that at the top of the hierarchy of gods are Brahma (the Creator), Vishnu (the Preserver), and Shiva (the Destroyer). Hindus believe that the human spirit is reincarnated many times, meaning that it is born into many bodies and lives many lives. Each time the soul comes to Earth, it becomes more and more religiously pure.

Eventually, the soul becomes as pure as the gods themselves and enters Saccidandanada (sach-ee-ahn-AHN-dah), a state of perfect spiritual existence that requires no further incarnations. As the soul travels through its incarnations, it is classified according to its religious purity into one of four groups called varnas (VAHR-nahs)—Brahmin (BRAH-min), Kshatriya (SHAH-tree-ah), Vaishya (VAISH-yah), or Sudra (SOO-drah). These varnas are ranked, with Brahmin at the top. Within each varna are a number of subdivisions called castes. Although the caste system was not maintained among immigrants to Guyana, East Indians continue to recognize those born in the Brahmin group

Guyanese Hindus offer morning prayers in a Lord Vishnu temple in Georgetown.

As with Awacaipu, other Amerindians traveled to missions and learned about other religions. One of these, a Makushí from the savanna region, brought back stories at the end of the nineteenth century of a god named Papa (as in "Father") who lived in the sky. He had a vision in which Papa told him to start a new religion called Hallelujah and spread it. Other groups picked up parts of the religion from the Makushí. One ritual, the thanksgiving ceremony, is still being practiced in the interior.

When hunters return with a good catch, they gather the animals and fish inside a hut that has been cleansed with water. Then they form a column outside the hut and begin to chant and drum to Papa, singing and dancing to songs and prayers taught by the Hallelujah prophets. When they have nearly reached the hut, they form a line, each man with his hand on his neighbor's shoulder, kneel, and pray to thank Papa for giving them a successful hunt. This is clearly a combination of native and Christian elements. Ironically, when missionaries reached the interior, they failed to recognize this ceremony as partly Christian and tried to ban it.

as the only legitimate religious leaders for their community. As the purest souls, only Brahmins can be pandits, or priests, of the Hindu religion.

Arya Samaj, or Reform Hinduism, was started in India in 1875 by Swami Dayanand Saraswati. The main differences between the two schools are that the reformists reject many of the practices of the Orthodox religion as superficial. For example, Arya Samaj Hinduism preaches that the three major gods—Brahma, Vishnu, and Shiva—are different facets of one god and that the minor gods are not gods at all, only humans who reached a high state of religious purity. For Reformists, worship involves meditation and yoga, rather than making offerings to idols or statues of the gods. The Reformists do not believe that a person is born into a varna. Rather they argue that a person becomes a member of one of the varnas as a result of his or her actions on Earth, so that a very virtuous person can become Brahmin.

MUSLIMS A minority of the Indo-Guyanese are followers of Islam, a religion started by Prophet Muhammad in Arabia in the seventh century CE.

THE FIVE PILLARS OF FAITH

Muslim religious practice is based on the "Five Pillars of Faith." These rules determine daily religious practice and inspire the major celebrations of the religion.

- The First Pillar of Faith is that there is only one true god, Allah, and Muslims must affirm this in their daily practice. This revelation was given to Muhammad on the "night of power," about ten days before the end of the month of Ramadan. This is celebrated in Muslim homes as Laylat al-Qadr.

- The Second Pillar of Faith is that Muslims must worship Allah five times a day.

- The Third Pillar of Faith is that every Muslim must distribute charity to the poor. Although this can be done at any time of the year, there is a special celebration for it called the Feast of Sacrifice, or Eid al-Adha. This is one of the officially recognized Islamic holidays in Guyana.

- The Fourth Pillar of Faith is that all Muslims should fast during the month of Ramadan. This is the month when the Quran, or the Muslim holy book, was revealed to Prophet Muhammad. To show respect, Muslims do not eat or drink during the daylight hours. The family comes together to eat in the evenings. Eid al-Fitr, or the Feast of Fast-Breaking, marks the end of Ramadan. This is the most joyous family celebration in the Islamic calendar, when everyone comes together to feast and celebrate the end of the fast.

- The Fifth Pillar of Faith is the hajj, or religious pilgrimage to Mecca, a holy city in Saudi Arabia. Every Muslim must try to make the trip once in his or her life.

Islam has spread around the world, especially to the east, from its origins in the Middle East. Muslims believe in one god, Allah. Their holy book, written in Arabic, is called the Quran. Muslim men attend prayer meetings in mosques. Women do not enter mosques, although they must pray regularly. The Muslim holy day is Friday, and Muslim holy men are called imams. Although Hindus and Muslims in India have had a long history of ethnic strife and have even fought a civil war, relations between the groups in Guyana are generally amicable.

OBEAH   Some Afro-Guyanese practice a folk religion called obeah (OH-bay-ah) based on African beliefs. Believers practice magic and believe that obeah priests have special powers drawn from traditional African gods and spirits. Obeah is based partly on the African concept that the ancestors have spirits that can affect the lives of the living and that relations between these two worlds have to be kept in good order. Practitioners wear charms or spells to protect themselves from harm. Obeah was made legal in 1970.

An indigenous Guyanan dresses in traditional clothing in the Shanklands Rainforest on the Essequibo River.

INDIGENOUS BELIEFS   Among Amerindians, there are a number of indigenous beliefs. Over the centuries, and still today, Amerindians have faced intense pressure from missionaries to convert to Christianity as part of the "civilizing" process.

Sometimes this pressure has had disastrous consequences, as in the case of the millennial movement started by Awacaipu, a shaman of the Arekuna tribe. Shamans play a significant role as healers and advisers to their villages. They are sought out to detect sorcery and combat evil. Some groups have remained more isolated and have managed to maintain their belief systems. They have pantheistic religions. The gods are usually represented by natural phenomena, such as waterfalls, and animals, like the jaguar. Amerindian religion stresses

Jim Jones brought his People's Temple to Guyana in 1974 with plans to set up an agricultural commune in the northwest of the country. Since this was territory disputed and possibly threatened by the Venezuelans, and because Jones claimed to be a friend of President Jimmy Carter, Burnham allowed the People's Temple to buy 3,800 acres (1,500 ha) of land in northwest Guyana. There, Jones established his commune deep in the jungle, away from any other village, and named it Jonestown.

Most of the followers of the People's Temple of Christ were African Americans, and Jones, who was white, committed the cult's full support to Burnham's dictatorship. Perhaps that was why the cult was allowed to import drugs and weapons with no interference from the authorities.

The cult came to international attention in 1978 when US Congressman Leo Ryan flew to Guyana along with a party of US government officials, concerned relatives, and members of the media. He announced that he was going to Jonestown to investigate claims that people in the group were being abused and held against their will.

After days of negotiations and interviews with members of the People's Temple, Ryan arranged for his party to fly out of Guyana on November 18, 1978, along with fourteen cult members who wished to leave. However, as one of the two small planes was taxiing to take off, a cult member posing as a defector opened fire on the passengers. Outside, on the runway, other People's Temple members began firing on the other plane, killing Ryan and four other people.

Later that day, back in Jonestown, Jones convinced or compelled 914 of his followers to take cyanide in a mass suicide. The cyanide was put into a purple juicelike beverage made from a powdered drink mix. Of the victims, 304 were infants or children. Some members of the cult, presumably those unwilling to drink the poison, were found murdered. Until the September 11, 2001, terror attacks, the Jonestown massacre was the largest single loss of American civilian life in a deliberate act.

One legacy of this dreadful event is that the popular phrase "drink the Kool-Aid" came into use. It means to follow blindly, or to show unquestioning obedience or loyalty to someone or something dangerous.

a respectful relationship between humans and the gods, who are evident in natural forms.

CULT GROUPS

Cults are pseudo-religious groups that indoctrinate their members into total loyalty and obedience to their leaders. They can be very dangerous to society if their intentions are not honorable. Under the Burnham dictatorship, Guyana was home to two such cults, both started by Americans. The more famous of these to the outside world was the People's Temple of Christ, led by Jim Jones.

The second cult group is less known outside Guyana but had devastating effects on politics within the country. It was called the House of Israel and was started by David Hill, an African American wanted by the FBI for a number of crimes. He fled the United States in 1972 and arrived in Guyana—two years before Jim Jones—where he became the Rabbi Edward Washington.

Under the cover of religion and dictatorship, these cults were given the right to operate in Guyana despite their illegal activities. Though both cults were led by Americans, their unsavory actions greatly influenced Guyana's reputation worldwide. The Guyanese people naturally don't want a repeat of this situation in the future.

Jim Jones raises his fist in a black power salute while preaching.

CHURCH AND STATE

Under the constitution, all Guyanese enjoy freedom of religion. There is no official state religion. Nevertheless, the major religious organizations have tended to associate themselves with political parties and have become quite involved in the daily political life in the country. There are both Hindu and Islamic religious associations that have openly sided with both major parties,

David Hill, a.k.a. "Rabbi" Edward Washington, convinced Guyanese dictator Forbes Burnham that he was a political refugee escaping a racist campaign against him.

Hill's cult, the House of Israel, was founded on the belief that blacks were the original Jews and had the right to occupy Israel. Claiming to be the Prophet Elijah, "Rabbi Washington" attracted mainly poor and uneducated Afro-Guyanese. Cult followers were indoctrinated to believe in the supremacy of blacks over other groups and to prepare for the day when other groups would be killed. Soon there were about eight thousand members throughout Guyana, and they were protected from the law by their close ties to Burnham's People's National Congress (PNC). Cult members wore uniforms in the colors of the PNC—black, red, and green. The group was essentially a private army—that is, thugs—used by the government to brutally disrupt legal strikes and harass people perceived to be in opposition to the dictatorship.

On July 14, 1979, a cult member named Bilal Ato killed an English Jesuit priest and photographer for the Catholic Standard *newspaper, Father Bernard Drake, in full view of spectators. Burnham refused to investigate the murder. It took three years to bring Ato to court, where he was defended by a state prosecutor and received a lighter sentence than his actions demanded. Walter Rodney, a prominent Guyanese historian, writer, and political activist, was one of the few who openly denounced the crime and accused the government of being behind it. Rodney was assassinated in 1980.*

The cult continued to function as long as Burnham lived. After his death, the government of his successor tried to soften the dictatorship and arrested cult leaders for crimes committed years earlier. In July 1986, Washington and some of his key associates were charged with the murder of Drake. After pleading guilty to the lesser charge of manslaughter, Washington received a fifteen-year prison sentence, but he was released in 1992. David Hill, a.k.a. Washington, died in New Jersey in 2001.

the PNC and the PPP, although the Indo-Guyanese have traditionally supported the PPP. The most vocal critics of the PNC dictatorship were the Christian churches and their umbrella organization, the Guyana Council of Churches (GCC). Today, with less political tension, church groups have been able to relax their pressure on the government.

FOLK BELIEFS

Besides formal religions, there are a number of folk traditions in Guyana. One in particular has captured the imagination of all ethnic groups. Stories about Anansi, a spider god from the Ashanti culture in West Africa, delight children of all backgrounds. Anansi, or Nancy as he is known in Guyana, is popular throughout the Caribbean. He is a trickster god, who is neither good nor evil. In the stories, he gets himself in trouble and uses his quick intelligence to escape. One of his archenemies is the tiger. Some people have linked these stories to slave life, arguing that Nancy represents the slave, who is weak and must use cunning to survive, and the tiger represents the master, who is strong.

INTERNET LINKS

http://www.globalreligiousfutures.org/countries/guyana
This site provides a statistical overview of religion in Guyana.

https://www.guyanatimesinternational.com/?p=49982
The *Guyana Times* marks the fortieth anniversary of the Jonestown murder-suicide by providing a Guyanese perspective on the event.

https://www.nytimes.com/1979/10/21/archives/black-supremacist-heads-guyana-cult-opposition-groups-say-followers.html
A *New York Times* article from 1979 provides a portrait of Rabbi Washington and the House of Israel.

https://www.state.gov/j/drl/rls/irf/2010_5/168218.htm
This is the US government report on religion in Guyana.

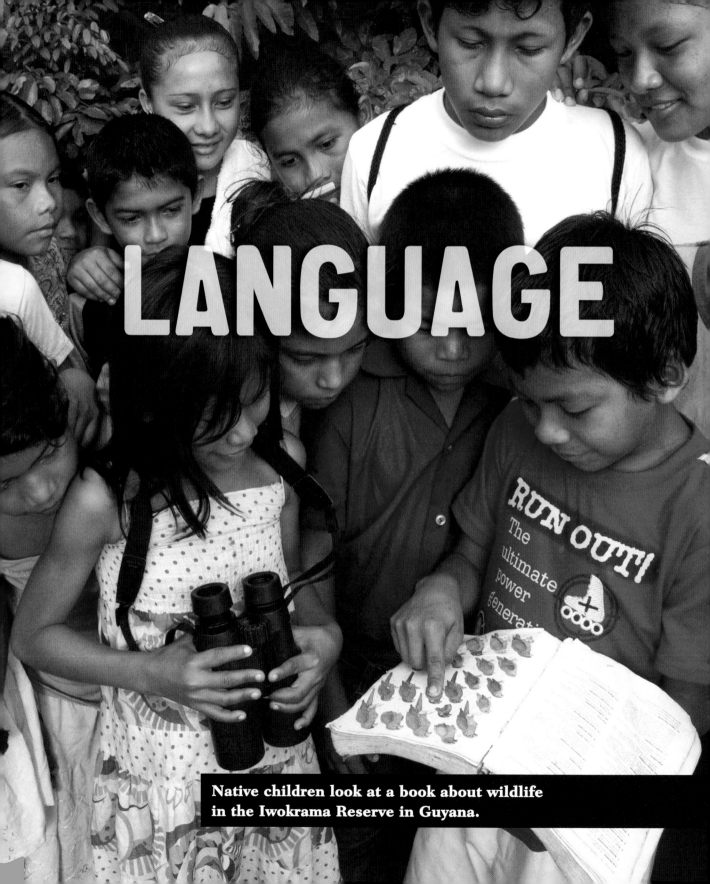

LANGUAGE

Native children look at a book about wildlife in the Iwokrama Reserve in Guyana.

9

E NGLISH IS THE OFFICIAL LANGUAGE of Guyana, making the country an anomaly on the predominantly Spanish-speaking South American continent. Geographically, Guyana is part of South America, but culturally and historically it has more in common with English-speaking Caribbean islands such as Trinidad and Tobago. In fact it is often classified with the Caribbean countries as part of the geographical region known as the Caribbean Basin.

The reasons for this confusion in regional identity are many. To begin with, the Guianas (French, Dutch, and British) were the only non-Spanish and non-Portuguese colonies on the South American mainland. They are small and are dwarfed by their much larger Spanish- and Portuguese-speaking neighbors, Venezuela and Brazil. When people think of South America, they rarely remember that not all of it is actually part of Latin America.

Guyana's colonial heritage and modern linguistic and cultural makeup make the nation "feel" more Caribbean than anything else, and this sense of identity is perhaps more important than the technicalities of

The Guyanese Creole language was long thought to be a corrupted or uneducated form of English. However, many linguists today say it's a legitimate language unto itself. It should not be viewed as a bastardization of English or as an inferior form of it. That view is now regarded as racist or ethnocentric.

Before the arrival of Europeans, most indigenous groups in the Amazon Basin and surrounding region relied on small-scale farming, hunting, and fishing. For this reason, they are usually classified first by language family rather than by distinct economic practices.

"Carib" refers to a family of related languages rather than to one single language. Carib-speaking people are thought to have come from an area in the Amazon River valley, now in modern Brazil. They began to migrate northward around 1200 CE, and by 1300 they were expanding into the Lesser Antilles (part of the islands of the Caribbean). There they intermarried with members of another language family, the Arawak. In this process, Carib was lost, so that by the time Europeans encountered indigenous people on the islands, they spoke only Arawak languages. Carib speakers remained on the mainland in northern Venezuela, the Guianas, and parts of Brazil.

Arawak speakers also inhabited parts of the mainland and were trying to expand along the northern coast of South America before European settlement. The third language group is Warrau. People of this group are found today between the Orinoco River in Venezuela and the Pomeroon River in Guyana. This is a swampy region, and it has been postulated that they moved here to escape the warlike Carib and Arawak speakers as the latter two groups expanded their territories.

geographical regions. In this way, language outweighs geography in giving the Guyanese their identity in the modern world.

GUYANESE CREOLE

In addition to English, many other languages are spoken in the country's homes and in the streets. The majority of the people also speak Guyanese, which is not a native language but a creole version of English.

A creole is a language that develops from the mixing and simplifying of different languages. Such languages often develop over time when people of different languages live near one another and need to communicate. In Guyana, Creole English contains many influences from the other people and cultures that have contributed to Guyanese life and history.

For example, Dutch words that are still used today include *koker* (KOH-ker), which means "water gate," and *stelling* (STEL-ling), a "wharf" or "quay." Not surprisingly these words describe things that were originally introduced and built by the Dutch.

Although the French occupied Guyana for only a short time around the turn of the eighteenth century, they left a linguistic heritage in the word for "rowboat," *bateau* (BAH-toh). Portuguese migrants have also left their linguistic mark in everyday language. Apart from some words for foods, there are also words such as *briga* (BREE-gah), used to describe someone who wants to fight, and *olhado* (ohl-YAH-doh), which means "evil eye." Chinese immigrants have mainly influenced the language with terms for food.

There are dozens of Amerindian words in use, particularly as place names, since these people were the first to settle the territory. Other Amerindian words include *warishi* (wahr-EE-shee), which refers to a basketwork backpack, and *benab* (BEN-ahb), meaning "hut." From the languages of the Indian people who made the voyage to Guyana, words such as *typee* (TY-pee), meaning "a strong love," and *carahi* (kah-rah-HEE), referring to a type of stewing pan, have entered everyday speech.

Amerindian schoolchildren of various ages attend class in the remote village of Surama in central Guyana.

Guyana and its cities have been called by many different names throughout their long history. The basis for the name Guyana came from the Amerindian name for the whole region—Guiana. This word means "land of many waters," an accurate description of this area, as there are close to 7,000 square miles (18,130 sq km) of inland water besides 285 miles (459 km) of the Atlantic Ocean fronting its coast.

Georgetown has also gone by different names. Although it was founded by the English, the French were the first to name it, calling the settlement "Longchamps." When the Dutch took it back from their French allies, they named it "Stabroek," and the old town market is still known by this name. When the English took back Guyana for good, they renamed their colonial capital "Georgetown" after a British monarch.

Inhabitants have also called their city "Mudtown," which describes what used to happen to the streets after the seasonal rains. A map of Guyana shows the influences of various cultures. There are names left over from the Dutch and English, such as New Amsterdam and Queenstown, and others that have come from Amerindians, such as Roraima and Kaieteur.

Some words from African languages have also come down through the generations, including *te-te* (teh-teh), a type of skin disease, and *kerreh* (KEH-reh), a state of power. Some common expressions in Creole English include *aw right*, which means "hello" and "okay"; *me no know*, which means "I don't know"; and *just now*, which means anything from "right away" to some time much later.

OTHER LANGUAGES

Although English is the official language and Creole English is the language spoken by most people on the streets, other languages are still spoken in the home and within certain ethnic communities. Another creole language, found only in Berbice, is a Dutch Creole left behind after many years of Dutch colonial occupation of the country. Sometimes just called "Berbice," this language is nearing extinction as its speakers die. It is a combination of

Areas such as the Caribbean Basin and the Guianas were ideal for the development of creole languages because so many people speaking so many different languages and dialects were brought together to work on plantations. Although the dominant linguistic influence was that of the master class, workers of African, Asian, and other descents were able to influence the language they used among themselves on the estates. For this reason, there are French, English, and Dutch Creoles in the Guianas.

Because creoles are young languages, they often have relatively simple vocabularies. As a result, many people mistakenly assume that they are not true languages and undervalue their cultural significance. In fact, creoles are just as rich as other traditional languages, and people who speak them can express as much of a range of meaning and subtlety as any person speaking a traditional language. Creoles are increasingly becoming the language of postcolonial literature and thought in countries where they are prevalent.

Dutch, Amerindian, and a Nigerian language. Another dying Dutch Creole is found in the Essequibo region and is known as Skepi. About half the words are similar to the words found in Berbice, but speakers claim that the two languages can't be mutually understood.

In many Indo-Guyanese homes, you can still hear one of the two main Indian languages that were spoken by the original immigrants—Hindi or Urdu—as well as Caribbean Hindustani, a dialect of Hindi. These are the languages spoken by the majority of the people. The Amerindian minority also speaks a number of languages and dialects based on the three main language/culture groupings found there—Arawak, Carib, and Warrau. Some specific Amerindian languages and dialects include Akawáio, Kalihna, Makushí, Patamona, Pemon, Waiwai, and Wapishana.

FOLK WISDOM AND PROVERBS

One heritage that is particularly African is the use of proverbs in regular speech. Because they were not allowed to have formal educations or write, slaves passed on their cultural values through the oral tradition of storytelling. This

VOICE OF THE PEOPLE: THE *CATHOLIC STANDARD*

Under the dictatorship of Forbes Burnham (in office 1964–1985), all significant print media were controlled by the ruling or opposition political parties, the PNC or the PPP. The notable exception was the Catholic Standard, *the only independent voice that tried to report the news accurately with no party bias. The paper was published and edited by Catholic priests, many of whom risked their lives to report and publish the news.*

Under the Jesuit priest Harold Wong, who became the editor in 1967, the paper took on a strong pro-democracy voice, which brought it into conflict with the Burnham administration. After writing an editorial critical of the presidential elections in 1973, Wong was ordered to resign by the angered Guyanese government. However, he refused.

In 1976, Andrew Morrison took over as editor of the paper and pushed it to an even more radical oppositional political stance. Under Morrison, the paper courageously defied censorship, investigated high-level corruption, and stood up for justice. Many staff members, mostly priests, faced death threats, and some, such as Michael James, an assistant editor in 1979, were assaulted. Photographer Bernard Drake was stabbed to death in 1979—Morrison was probably the intended victim—by a member of the cult House of Israel, very likely on behalf of the government. These men performed an invaluable public service, bravely bringing the news to Guyana and financing the paper with international donations.

Today, the Catholic Standard *is still published, but under much improved democratic conditions. As such, it has switched its focus away from political topics and back to Catholic religious concerns. It has a circulation of about fourteen thousand.*

is still evident today in the many proverbs that people use to communicate with one another. Proverbs are short metaphors that capture an essential idea about right and wrong or a story about how the world works.

An example of an Afro-Guyanese proverb, written in Creole English, is, "Cat foot soft but he ah scratch bad." This means, "Be careful; some friendly-seeming people may turn around and hurt you." Another is "Big tree fall down, goat bite he leaf," meaning, "When a great man falls, he is no longer to be feared." "Baby who ah cry ah house and ah door ah same thing" means, "Treat other children the same way you treat your own."

THE MEDIA

The media in Guyana is largely government owned. The state-owned TV Channel 11, the National Communication Network (NCN), provides limited service and supplements the two satellite relay stations that bring US television to Guyanese audiences. The NCN also operates the radio stations Voice of Guyana, Fresh FM, and Hot FM. Government limits on licensing of new private radio stations have restricted competition in broadcast media

In the print media, the government owns one daily newspaper, the *Guyana Chronicle*. There are two other private dailies, the *Stabroek News* and the *Kaieteur News.* All three papers operate online news sites.

There are about 262,425 internet users in Guyana, about 35.7 percent of the population (according to a 2016 estimate). This figure is likely to increase as service providers compete for subscribers.

A Guyanese man in Linden, Guyana, holds a local newspaper.

INTERNET LINKS

https://www.bbc.com/news/world-latin-america-19546912
The BBC provides a short overview of Guyana's media.

http://www.guyana.org/proverbs.html
This site lists some Guyanese proverbs as expressed in Guyanese Creole.

https://guyanachronicle.com/2013/06/17/creolese-a-language-all -of-its-own
This article takes a good look at the linguistic creativity and validity of the Guyanese Creole language.

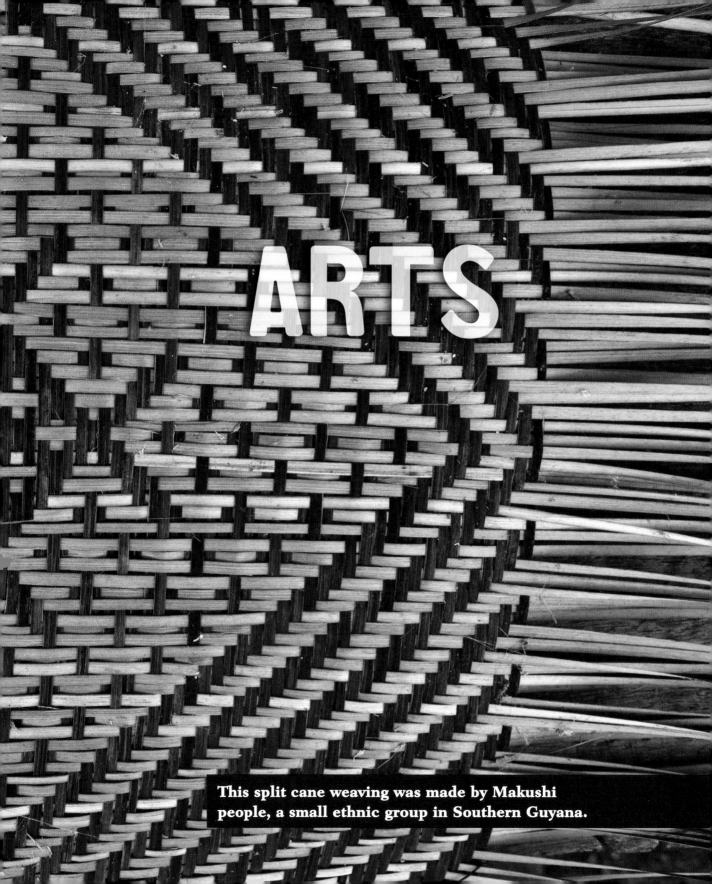

ARTS

This split cane weaving was made by Makushi
people, a small ethnic group in Southern Guyana.

10

T RUE TO ITS CARIBBEAN IDENTITY, Guyana has a vibrant popular arts culture that reflects its multiethnic population in a kaleidoscope of expression. The country's proximity to the West Indies, particularly Trinidad and Tobago, can be heard in its lively Calypso music and dance—as well as in other Afro-Caribbean music genres. Guyana's East Indian people bring a South Asian thread to the culture, and Amerindian artisans add an indigenous flavor. Meanwhile, the British and European colonial influence can still be seen in Old World architecture.

VISUAL ARTS

The Timehri rock paintings, probably the oldest art in Guyana, are one of the nation's most valuable Amerindian legacies. Located on a quartz cliff face near Imbaimadai (on the Karowrieng River, a tributary of the Mazaruni in western Guyana), the rock paintings (petroglyphs) are a collection of roughly painted animals, symbols, and handprints that are believed to date back to 1300 CE.

"Tumatumari" by Aubrey Williams, is part of the *Timehri* series of murals at the Cheddi Jagan International Airport in Guyana. *Timehri* is an Amerindian word meaning "mark of the hand," or "rock paintings" and is the name of a village in Guyana.

Some of the animals portrayed include sloths, accurately depicted hanging upside down from a vine, and anteaters. There are also abstract symbols such as squares, zigzags, and strings of lozenges (diamond shapes). At the base of the cliff, there are hundreds of handprints in red paint. There are so many of these that they overlap. Although these are clearly the work of prehistoric Amerindians, modern Amerindians in the area have a different story to explain Timehri. They say that the paintings were done by their supreme god, Amalivaca, who visited the area during a great flood. The paintings extend over an area that is 50 feet (15 m) wide and 25 feet (7.6 m) high and are so impressive that the name of this cliff was chosen for Guyana's international airport when it was renamed after independence.

Aubrey Williams (1926–1990), one of Guyana's best-known modern painters, also drew inspiration from the Amerindian past and present. He claimed to have Amerindian blood and came to know the Warrau people quite well when he served as an agricultural officer in their district. He spent two years with the Warrau and was even initiated into their tribe. His paintings reflect his knowledge of Guyana's interior, with its steamy primeval forests and powerful rivers. Other Guyanese painters include Donald Locke and Denis Williams, who moved to Europe to paint and write.

ARCHITECTURE

Guyana's older cities and towns are notable for their distinctive architecture. The oldest and most valued buildings are all made of wood. The coast was originally forested, so there was an abundant supply of this material. However, pine was often imported for construction because it reacted to the tropical climate better than some of the locally available hardwoods. Pine was also easier to work with when carpenters did not have power tools, and it was light enough to not sink into the alluvial mud of the coast.

Wooden houses in Georgetown are typical of the city's architectural style.

Guyanese houses combined European styles and the demands of the local environment. Because stone or concrete structures would have sunk into the mud, even large public buildings had to be made of wood. Some incredible feats of engineering were accomplished in Georgetown. Saint George's Cathedral, for example, is the tallest wooden church in the world. Its spire reaches 143 feet (43.5 m) into the air.

This may not seem very high when one considers the concrete and steel skyscrapers of today, but to try to build something so high without a system of reinforcement (such as steel beams) or a deep basement is not easy. Guyana's colonial architects and carpenters managed to overcome this difficulty. Although much of their work has been destroyed by termites and fire over the years, there are still some impressive examples of this distinctly Guyanese art and craftsmanship.

As various generations of Guyanese adapted to living on the hot, humid, and flood-prone coast, a number of architectural innovations helped make life cooler, drier, and safer. The first innovation in colonial housing was to copy local Amerindian designs and build the house on stilts. This kept the home out of the mud and away from flood waters. The area beneath the house could be used for animals or storage.

Until very recently, houses were all made of wood. They were oriented to take advantage of the winds blowing from the northeast off the ocean. There were also special windows and shutters called Demerara windows. These are shutters that are hinged at the top and built out from the wall of the house. Between the shutter and the wall are moldings with decorative cut-out designs and a small tray at the base.

The holes in the moldings allowed for the passage of air, while the tray was used by wealthier houseowners for blocks of ice so that when the breeze blew over the ice, it would become cooler and thus cool the room inside. Ice was brought from North America and was stored in sawdust or sand until needed. The front of the house was dominated by a covered veranda that had shutters and jalousies to allow air to circulate. A jalousie is a system of louvers that can be set at different angles. In this way, the whole wall was open to the sea breezes.

The kitchen was always built in the back of the house in a separate, concrete-reinforced room. This was because wood stoves were the most common way to cook and presented a fire hazard in wooden homes. The demands of safety and a hot climate created typical Guyanese houses, which today are still an attractive feature of older sections of Georgetown.

MUSIC

Music is perhaps Guyana's richest cultural treasure. All the different groups have contributed their musical sense and instruments to Guyana's national musical repertoire. For example, Portuguese immigrants brought both their *rajaos* (rah-JOWZ; a type of banjo) and *braggas* (BRAH-gahs; small guitars) with them to the new land. One type of music that has been credited to them is *santapee* (SAHN-tah-pee) music.

Probably the most common element in Guyanese music is the drum. Amerindian religious ceremonies, such as the hallelujah rite, depend on the drum to set the rhythm and keep the beat. The Afro-Guyanese still use the drum extensively in a variety of musical forms. One of the better-known types of music to come out of Guyana and other Caribbean countries is that of the steel band, whose drums are traditionally made from old oil barrels that have been tuned to produce different musical notes.

The Guyana Music Festival was held biannually from 1957 to 1979. Neglected for close to thirty years, the festival was successfully relaunched in 2007 and continues annually. Local people as well as Caribbean artists gather to perform various music styles such as soca, calypso, shanto, and reggae. Vocal solos, duets, verse speaking, choral speaking, school and church choirs, folk songs, steel pan players, and gospel groups all come together to make the festival an unforgettable experience.

The Indo-Guyanese have also brought their traditional music and instruments, including the sitar, a stringed instrument that must be placed on the floor to be played because it is so long. Traditional Indian music is often played to accompany dancing.

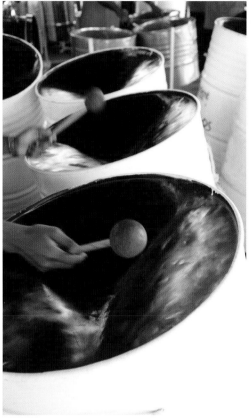

A musician plays steel drums at a festival in Georgetown.

DANCE

As with music, Guyana enjoys traditional dance forms from many lands.

Two distinctly African dances that made the crossing of the Atlantic and are still performed today are the *que-que* (kwe-kwe) and the *cumfa* (KUM-fah). The que-que is performed by groups at weddings and other public celebrations. The group splits into two, with each side asking and answering questions about the people involved in the event. This can be quite humorous for the participants and spectators. Cumfa is a quasi-religious dance accompanied by drumming. The participants dance in a rhythmic fashion until they begin to

Brought over by the indentured laborers many decades ago, Indian heritage continues to pervade Guyana's culture. In dance, the art form is divided into three distinct categories—classical, folk, and Bollywood, the movie musical style.

The kathak *(KAH-tahk), for example, is a traditional East Indian dance form performed by women. It is a highly stylized form of classical dance in which the dancers tell stories through rhythmic foot movements, hand gestures, and facial expressions, especially the eyes. These stories are typically legends from ancient mythology and great Indian epics, especially from the life of Lord Krishna.*

Classical dance requires years of training, but folk dance is easier for everyone to participate in. These dance forms are performed at festivals and celebrations.

fall into a trance. They believe that drums can summon supernatural forces and spirits that enter the bodies of the dancers. Cumfa is not performed as a public dance but in private among those who believe in the power of the drums and the dance.

CRAFTS

The Amerindian heritage and contribution is notable in Guyanese crafts. Indigenously produced crafts include basketry, floor mats, and chairs made of woven reeds and grasses. Amerindian hammocks from the interior are also highly prized.

These remarkable creations are extremely light and can expand to incredible widths because of the natural fibers used and the technique of weaving. The

A resident weaves a basket in a village in western Guyana.

sleeper can also use the extra material as a blanket so that the hammock becomes a complete bed. However, because hammocks take a long time to make, most Amerindian weavers prefer to keep them for personal use.

Other crafts produced in Guyana include brassware and gold filigree. Brass objects are made using a technique of beating or pounding the metal into shape. This takes not only skill but great strength and stamina, and results in beautiful bowls and trays. Gold is also worked into filigree jewelry. Filigree work is a technique where gold is rolled into fine wires, which are then shaped into intricate designs and patterns. The work is painstaking and must be done by hand.

Some of Guyana's valuable woods are also used in furniture production. Both the green and purple heartwood trees make sturdy and beautiful pieces. The most highly prized wood is wamara (wah-MAH-rah), a type of brown ebony that is very hard and durable.

LITERATURE

Aimé Césaire

The most significant trend in twentieth-century literature in the Caribbean and Guyana has been negritude. This term was coined by Aimé Césaire, a black intellectual from the Caribbean island of Martinique. Césaire, along with other thinkers from Africa and Léon-Gontran Damas from Guyana, were students in Paris in the 1930s. This talented group was especially interested in the work of other black artists and writers and started a trend toward awareness of ethnicity and history in the arts. Negritude was a poetic term that was meant to stress the significance and beauty of black art from both Africa and the New World.

One of the writers who most inspired this group and their successors in the negritude tradition was René Maran of Guyana. Maran's novel *Batouala* (published in 1921) was openly anticolonialist and written from the black viewpoint. It caused quite a scandal in literary circles but also won the Prix Goncourt, a renowned French literary prize. In response to the anticolonial debate surrounding Maran's work, the students formed an anticolonialist magazine called *Légitime Défense* (Legitimate Defense) that was published from 1932 to 1934 in Paris. From then on, negritude and black pride were significant forces in the literature of the Caribbean.

Not all of Guyana's modern writers were influenced by Parisian culture. Edgar Mittelholzer sought the roots of his colonial identity in London, which he visited in the 1940s. His most famous work is *Morning at the Office*, published in 1950. Other writers include Wilson Harris, whose works include two books based on the oral traditions of the Carib and Arawak Amerindians, *The Sleepers of Roraima* (1970) and *The Age of the Rainmakers* (1971), and a novel about travels to the interior during Guyana's colonial period, *Palace of the Peacock* (1960).

Other writers, such as Denis Williams, found their inspiration and cultural roots in Africa. Williams is famous for his book *Other Leopards* (1963). Karen King-Aribisala is remembered for winning two Commonwealth Book Awards

(Africa Region) for *Our Wife and Other Stories* (1991) and *The Hangman's Game* (2008), which is based on the heroic revolt by African slaves against their British colonial masters in 1823.

A memorable addition to the historical tradition of negritude was Guyana's Walter Rodney. His academic and journalistic contributions to Guyana were cut short. He was killed by a bomb in his car while running for office in the election of 1980.

INTERNET LINKS

https://www.stabroeknews.com/2010/guyana-review/04/29/architecture-building-under-our-sun
This news site offers an in-depth article on housing design in Guyana.

https://www.stabroeknews.com/2016/sunday/arts-on-sunday/07/31/what-is-african-dance
"What Is African Dance?" offers insight into the art form.

LEISURE

A young boy swings the bat in a street cricket match in Georgetown.

11

THE GUYANESE PEOPLE ARE generally not wealthy, but they still have many options for entertainment in the home and community. Family plays an important role in many leisure activities. Many folks also participate in sports and have inherited one of their most popular games, cricket, from the British.

MAKING LIFE

In Guyana, a distinction is made between "making a living" and "making life." These two expressions refer to the two aspects of life that the Guyanese consider essential. The first, "making a living," has the same meaning as it does in standard English and refers to working in order to provide food and other essentials for oneself and one's family. The second phrase, "making life," refers to socializing and taking care of other members of the family and the wider community. Making life can mean anything from chatting with a neighbor to lending a hand when needed or participating in village or community events.

Both aspects of life, the economic and the social, are highly valued, and the Guyanese strive to maintain a balance between them. It is considered unhealthy to focus more on making a living and to ignore making life. People who are perceived as doing this are considered to be greedy and antisocial. Likewise, people who only make life without working to make

The West Indies were the official hosts of the 2007 Cricket World Cup, and Guyana hosted six Super Eight matches as part of the series. The fifteen-thousand-seat Providence Stadium in Georgetown, also referred to as Guyana National Stadium, was built specifically for that purpose.

Stabroek market, the largest marketplace in Georgetown, is a popular place to browse and shop.

a living are called "limers" or are said to be "liming." This means that they are living off their friends and relatives and are not pulling their economic weight. There are a number of ways of making life in Guyana.

One of the most popular pastimes available to all Guyanese is going to the local store or marketplace to chat with neighbors. Older men with time on their hands, especially, gather at popular spots in town to talk with each other. No other activity is necessary to make this a satisfying leisure activity. Younger men can often be found at bars, called "rum houses," where they meet to share a drink and play dominoes. Although women are not traditionally part of these male groups, they too meet to share the day's news, often at the market, where they may be engaged in selling produce.

In Georgetown, there are several more recreational options. The Botanical Gardens and the seawall are popular for taking a stroll in the cool evening. Both of these public parks have bandstands where the Police Force and Defense Force bands sometimes play for the public. In addition, there are cinemas, museums, and theaters. Swimming in the ocean along the most populated stretches of the coast, however, is not popular because of the pollution from the drainage ditches and the silt from rivers and seawalls.

There are some ethnic differences in how people entertain themselves. For Afro-Guyanese youth, one of the most popular ways to spend a weekend evening is to go to a dance. Many villages have community centers where dances are held regularly, and towns often have mobile discos (movable sound systems) that can be hired for any event.

Among Indo-Guyanese, public dancing is not so popular because young women are not supposed to go out without a chaperone. However, people of all ages enjoy going to the cinema to catch the latest Bollywood movie. There is also a religion-based social event called a *jhag*.

At certain times in life, people want to give thanks for the happiness and good fortune they have experienced. Hindus do not have a single thanksgiving day to do this, but they can hold small family thanksgivings called jhags (JAGs) whenever there is a reason. For example, when a child is born, and later has his or her first haircut, jhags are held by families who can afford them to celebrate and give thanks.

This festivity is nominally religious in nature, since a pandit is hired to read from the holy books and talk about religious matters. However, jhags are also social occasions when members of the extended family gather to socialize and celebrate successes in the family. Jhags can last up to five days and are accompanied by singing and feasting. A jhag is a social as well as a religious event and is a part of making life.

Children gather after school to play various games together. They especially enjoy activities such as kite-flying and simple games that they make up. They also play some of the sports that are popular in Guyana, such as cricket, field hockey, basketball, and soccer. Guyanese people of all ages enjoy singing and music as part of their social activities. There is a large repertoire of popular songs and music, and even songs just for children or for parties. Storytelling is a traditional pastime that is dying out as more people turn to radio and television for home entertainment.

SPORTS

By far the most popular sport in Guyana is cricket. This game originated in England hundreds of years ago and spread to most British colonies, including the West Indies. Guyana is one of the countries that has always contributed players to the West Indies team. Famous Guyanese cricketers include Lance Gibbs, Roy Fredericks, and Clive Lloyd.

In recent times, the main heroes have been locals Carl Hooper and Shivnarine Chanderpaul, who hail from the Bourda Georgetown Cricket Club. Founded in Guyana in 1858, it is also the longest-surviving cricket club in the entire Caribbean.

Cricket is a ball-and-bat game that is popular in England and in former British colonies where children learned to play the game in colonial schools. The rules of the game are rather complicated and can be difficult for nonplayers to understand.

Basically, the game is played by two teams of eleven players each. They play on an oval field. In the middle of the field is a rectangle called a pitch. There are two wickets, one at either end of the pitch. A wicket is a set of three posts, or stumps, in the ground on which are balanced two bails, or shorter sticks. Each team tries to keep its bails balanced on the stumps throughout the game. A bowler throws the ball, and a batsman uses a paddle-shaped bat to try to hit the ball into the field. Unlike in baseball, the batsman holds the bat quite low to defend the wicket that he stands in front of. If he hits the ball, he can score "runs," which are worth points in the game.

The batsman can be "dismissed" (similar to being "out" in baseball) from the game if the bowler hits the wicket with the ball, if a fielder catches the batted ball before it hits the ground (like catching a pop fly in baseball), if the batsman breaks the wicket with his own body or uses his body (instead of the bat) to defend the wicket, or if a member of the other team breaks the wicket while the batsman is attempting a "run."

Games are called matches, and they can last for days, since each inning is very long. An inning—there are only one or two in a match—ends when the tenth batsman is out, when a certain number of balls has been bowled, or when the batting team captain volunteers to end the inning. Players use padding to protect their legs from errant balls.

In June 2018, Guyana was named the Best First-Class Team of the Year at the annual Cricket West Indies Awards. That same year, the Emerging Cricketer of the Year went to twenty-year-old Guyanese player Keemo Paul, who plays for the West Indies team.

Soccer and baseball are also popular in Guyana. Another sport played with a ball and stick is field hockey. Field hockey sticks are rather different from ice hockey sticks, and a ball is used instead of a puck. Field hockey is often played by girls as well as boys. Other sports that enjoy some local club support are basketball, rugby (similar to American football), tennis, swimming, and karate.

Horse racing is a popular spectator sport. Races in Britain are broadcast in Guyana, and people love to bet on the horses. The local newspapers devote as much space to the races as they do to national politics. The Guyanese also like two other types of races—motor racing and goat racing. The Guyana Motor Racing Club holds international motorcycle and car races every March and October. Much less glamorous is goat racing, which is a local sport not found elsewhere.

A sport that attracts mainly foreigners is sport fishing. Although tourism is only now being promoted officially, the government has already acted to protect the environment and is discouraging the export of rare and endangered animal species.

INTERNET LINKS

https://www.britannica.com/sports/cricket-sport
This encyclopedia article offers information about the history of cricket.

https://guyanatimesgy.com/category/sports
Updates on regional sports news can be found on this media site.

https://www.kaieteurnewsonline.com/category/sports
Local sports are covered by this Guyanese news site.

FESTIVALS

An Easter kite soars to the sky. Kite flying on Easter weekend is a uniquely Guyanese tradition.

12

GUYANA'S CALENDAR OF PUBLIC holidays reflects its diverse population. Major Christian, Hindu, and Muslim festivals are recognized as national holidays. Two international holidays are New Year's Day and Labor Day, May 1. In addition, patriotic days honoring the country's history fill out the year.

CHRISTIAN FESTIVALS

The two most important celebrations in the Christian world are Christmas and Easter. Christmas marks the birth of Jesus and is celebrated on December 25 with family feasting and gift-giving. Easter, including Good Friday and Easter Monday, is a time to reflect on how Christ died for people's sins. Friday is the day he was crucified, and Sunday is when he was resurrected. Although these are Christian holidays, everyone in Guyana takes part in the festivities.

Christmas is one of the biggest celebrations in the country. Bands in costume called masquerade bands travel through the towns. The music is accompanied by limbo dancers. Limbo dancing is a Caribbean favorite that involves trying to bend over backward to dance below poles held at various heights by other people. The best limbo dancers are true acrobats,

In 2016, Guyana marked its fiftieth anniversary of independence with a Golden Jubilee celebration. The colorful parade of floats that is annually held on Mashramani in February was moved to Independence Day on May 26 for that year.

The Easter Bunny is a no-show in Guyana, but the children don't care. Although the foreign custom of coloring eggs has recently been catching on in the country, the real Easter thrill is up in the air. Who needs a rabbit when you have the beach, the ocean, and ... kites!

Kite flying is a beloved Guyanese Easter weekend tradition, a custom that dates back to the nineteenth century at least. The practice of kite flying itself probably came to Guyana with Chinese indentured laborers in the mid-1800s, but how it came to be associated with Easter is uncertain. Christians like to say the upward flights of the kites celebrate the resurrection of Jesus, which certainly makes sense metaphorically.

Because Easter is celebrated as a four-day weekend, people enjoy the extra time they get to spend with families and friends. In Georgetown it has become popular to go to the seawall to watch musical groups perform, and people of all religions take part in the kite-flying fun.

If that isn't enough, there is also the Bartica Regatta held on Easter weekend at the confluence of the Mazaruni, Cuyuni, and Essequibo Rivers. The event is much like a carnival, with a variety of water sports, a gospel fest, a beauty contest, a children's fair, and plenty of music, food, and drink.

since the objective is to avoid falling down or touching the pole. The music is produced by flutes and drums. People also visit each other's homes and wish one another Merry Christmas and Happy New Year. Pepperpot is a favorite Christmas dish—for breakfast!

HINDU FESTIVALS

Holi, or Phagwah, is a Hindu celebration of spring in India. Known as the "festival of colors," or "the festival of love," it's time for merriment, forgiveness, and thanksgiving. It's not a day to wear your best clothes, however. Outdoors, people toss colored powders on each other and drench each other with water from water guns and balloons. In Guyana, people of all backgrounds, not just Hindus, participate in the fun, and there is a big celebration in Georgetown.

Divali (Dewali, Deepavali), also known as the Festival of Lights, is an autumn holiday celebrated by Hindus around the world. It is a celebration in honor of Lakshmi, the goddess of wealth and prosperity. At this time, Lakshmi is said to return home from her summer residence in the mountains, and lights are lit to help her find her way. Another reason for the lights is the story of an Indian king, Lord Rama, who was banished from his kingdom for fourteen years. At the end of his banishment, he returned to reclaim his land, but it was the darkest night of the year, so the people lit up the night. Divali celebrates his return. This holiday may be celebrated on different dates, but it always falls in the month of October or November.

MUSLIM FESTIVALS

Islam follows a lunar calendar. This calendar is not synchronized with the standard Western calendar, so from one year to the next, important religious dates occur at different times. The Islamic calendar marks a number of important days based on the life of the Prophet Muhammad—who revealed the teachings of the religion to the people—and other significant dates in religious history. In Guyana, Eid al-Adha, the Feast of the Sacrifice, is a national holiday.

Muslims also celebrate the day of Muhammad's birth, called Youman Nabi, also known as Mawlid al-Nabi. This is also an official holiday in Guyana, although it is celebrated only within the Muslim community. There are special recitations about the life of Muhammad in the mosques and feasting among family members.

HISTORIC HOLIDAYS

There are four major historic holidays in Guyana.

MASHRAMANI   Also called Republic Day, it is observed on February 23. On that date in 1970, independent Guyana adopted a new constitution and declared itself a republic within the Commonwealth of Nations. The name Mashramani derives from an Amerindian word, and is often shortened to

Muslims believe that the Biblical prophets are the prophets of Allah (God). They respect these prophets and the stories of their lives. In the Genesis story of Ibrahim (Abraham, the patriarch of the three "Abrahamic" religions—Judaism, Christianity, and Islam) Allah asks Ibrahim to sacrifice his son Ishmael (in the Quran, he is named Ishmael; in the Bible, he is Isaac) to prove his faith. Ibrahim proceeds to do as he is commanded, but at the last moment, Allah provides a ram to be killed instead, and Ishmael remains unharmed.

Muslims believe Ishmael is an ancestor of Muhammad, so this story is very important to them. To celebrate the day of sacrifice, Muslims prepare meat to eat with their families and to give to the poor. This is also called the Great Feast (the Lesser Feast is Eid al-Fitr, which ends the holy month of Ramadan).

"Mash." Of all the historic holidays, this is the most festive. It is marked by such festivities as calypso contests, costume competitions, and picnics. The highlight of the day is a parade of floats. Companies sponsor the building of floats that follow different themes, and these are then brought together for a parade in Georgetown that is judged for best float. Many people participate in the construction and decorating of the floats, and many others come to watch the parade.

INDEPENDENCE DAY   May 26 marks the day that Guyana became free of British colonial rule in 1966. In 2016, Guyana celebrated fifty years of independence with a Golden Jubilee.

CARIBBEAN DAY   Also called CARICOM Day, this holiday is celebrated in early July. It's a time when people reflect on what it means to be part of CARICOM (the Caribbean Community) and celebrate Caribbean culture.

FREEDOM DAY   Also called Emancipation Day, this celebration in early August commemorates the emancipation of slaves in 1834. It is celebrated by games and African drumming. People also eat African foods on this day to celebrate the African contribution to Guyanese culture.

A CALENDAR OF OFFICIAL HOLIDAYS

New Year's Day . . . . January 1
Mashramani (Republic Day) . . . . February 23
Holi (Phagwah) . . . . February/March
Good Friday, Easter, Easter Monday. . . . . March/April
Labor Day . . . . May 1
Arrival Day . . . . May 5
Independence Day. . . . . May 26
CARICOM (Caribbean) Day . . . . first Monday in July
Emancipation Day . . . . August 1
Diwali (Deepavali). . . . . October/November
Christmas Day. December 25
Boxing Day. . . . . December 26
Eid al-Adha . . . . varies according to Islamic calendar
Youman Nabi (Prophet Muhammad's birthday) . . varies according to Islamic calendar

INTERNET LINKS

http://exploreguyana.org/event/phagwah
Guyana's celebration of Phagwah, or Holi, is described on this page.
Other festivals are also featured on this site.

**https://www.kaieteurnewsonline.com/2017/12/25/a-guyanese
-style-christmas**
The Guyanese news site describes a typical Christmas in the nation.

**https://www.npr.org/sections/thesalt/2014/12/24/372514524/
guyanese-christmas-gives-a-whole-new-meaning-to-slow-food**
This story explains the traditional Guyanese foods of Christmas.

https://www.timeanddate.com/holidays/guyana
This calendar site provides yearly dates for important holidays
in Guyana.

FOOD

A vendor's table is piled high with fresh vegetables at the Stabroek Market in Georgetown.

13

A FRICAN, AMERINDIAN, CARIBBEAN, Chinese, Creole, East Indian, European—all of these food cultures contribute to the cuisine of Guyana. Each group of people has brought something of their homeland and food preferences with them, and many of these "ethnic foods" have entered the standard repertoire of all Guyanese people. Stews and curries; cassava, yams, and other starchy root vegetables; hot peppers; and even a Guyanese-style chow mein are among the nation's popular foods

Some Guyanese staple foods go by charming names. Pepperpot, cook-up rice, *metemgee*, boil 'n fry, mango sour, and custard block are just a few of many dishes from various cultures that make up Guyanese cuisine.

AMERINDIAN TRADITIONS

Most of the Amerindian groups who still practice their traditional culture are horticulturists who clear small areas of land in the jungle to plant crops. Their staple crop is the cassava (manioc), a root crop that is native to the jungle. When cassava is raw, it contains prussic acid, which is poisonous to people. To remove the poison, Amerindian women first rub the root across a board studded with sharp stones. This grates the hard

A woman toasts cassava flour over an open flame.

tuber into shreds, which are then squeezed to remove the juice. The leftover pulp can then be ground into flour and used to make bread, which looks like a large pancake. This bread is cooked on large flat pans over a fire. Flatbreads do not contain yeast to make them rise.

The poisonous juices are boiled in ceramic pots so that the poison is absorbed by the clay. The bitter liquid that remains is cassareep, a flavoring used in Guyana's national dish, pepperpot. This is a type of meat-based stew that cooks for hours over an open fire with lots of pepper. It is often left out and reboiled for days. Cassava is also used to make a type of alcohol called *casiri* (KAH-see-ree).

SOMETHING FOR (AND FROM) EVERYONE

About 90 percent of the Guyanese live in the settled coastal strip. The many different cuisines in this area are a reflection of the variety of cultures that live there.

EAST INDIAN   The East Indians brought their curries and *dhals* (DAHLS) with them, and today many Guyanese consider these to be standard food in their homes. Favorite meat curries in Guyana are lamb, shrimp, and chicken. Dhals are stews made with legumes such as lentils. These, like curries, involve the blending of lots of flavors and are cooked for a long time. The customary accompaniment to curry and dhal is rice.

A popular festive food is "cook-up," which is any kind of meat prepared in coconut milk and served with rice and beans. Coconut milk requires a lot of labor to prepare and is very rich, so it is not eaten every day in most homes. Another Caribbean food that reflects an East Indian heritage is *roti* (ROH-tee). These are large turnovers made with a flatbread and filled with curried meats and potatoes.

CHINESE AND PORTUGUESE   Both the Chinese and Portuguese have also contributed to the Guyanese menu. Guyana boasts of some excellent Cantonese restaurants run by its Chinese inhabitants. Noodle dishes are very popular.

The Portuguese have contributed a variety of foods, including garlic pork, *bacalhau* (bah-cah-LAU,), *bolo do mel* (BOH-loh doh MAYL), garlic soup with egg, and couscous. Bacalhau is salted codfish and can be prepared in stews and soups. Bolo do mel is a cake made with molasses, a by-product of sugarcane processing. Couscous was probably brought to the islands of Madeira from North Africa, where it is a staple food, before making the journey to Guyana. It is a sort of granulated pasta made from cracked wheat, and can be flavored or plain.

Pumpkin is used as both a fruit and vegetable in Guyana, and the Portuguese fry it to make pumpkin fritters. As Catholics, the Portuguese observe Shrove Tuesday (the Tuesday before Lent begins) by eating special pancakes called *malassados* (mah-lah-SAH-dohs) and *sonhos* (SOHN-yohs).

AFRICAN   African heritage is apparent in the use of yams and okra in many dishes, including *callalu*. *Foo-foo* (foo-foo) comes directly from Africa and is a type of cake made from plantains. *Metemgee* (MEH-tam-gee) is another coconut milk—based stew that includes yams, cassava, and plantains.

OTHER FOODS

Because Guyana is a coastal country, seafood figures prominently in Guyanese kitchens. The best catches are shrimp, red snapper, and sea trout. All of these can be prepared in a number of ways and served with rice and peas. From the interior comes good quality beef and freshwater fish. Guyana also grows red and green peppers, green onions, eggplant, celery, avocados, tomatoes, and breadfruit.

DRINKS

As well as distinctive food, Guyana has several local drinks. The local beer, called Banks, has won many international awards. Banks is a brand that originated in Barbados but is produced locally in Georgetown too. A sugar-producing country, Guyana makes an excellent rum known as Demerara.

Children enjoy local soft drinks such as Banko Shandy, a ginger beer, and Malta Vita, another popular local beverage. Guyana also grows a variety of fruits that make delicious juices, including oranges, grapefruits, pineapples, mangoes, tangerines, and watermelons.

SHOPPING

Every city and town has a central market where most people shop for their food and other household needs. The largest of these is Stabroek Market in Georgetown, which was built by the Dutch. Here, sellers and buyers gather every day to haggle and bargain for food and other household supplies. Small producers of fruit and vegetables also ply the streets selling their wares or give them to children to sell after school.

Since many goods are imported into Guyana and therefore are often in short supply, people try to develop good relationships with local shopkeepers. Sometimes shopkeepers refuse to sell goods that are hard to get to people who are not their regular customers, or they insist that the customer buy something else at a higher price in order to get the scarce product.

The North American routine of driving to the supermarket, where everything is priced and in one place, has yet to catch on in Guyana. Most people prefer to buy their food fresh and to shop frequently during the week. They enjoy haggling over prices. This system is also more environmentally friendly, since most food is not packaged, and people bring their own shopping baskets rather than use plastic bags.

Colorful umbrellas shade the people and the produce at the Stabroek Market.

INTERNET LINKS

https://www.alicaspepperpot.com
This Guyanese cooking site has many recipes and uses American measurements.

http://guyanachronicle.com/2013/12/21/the-foods-we-like-at-christmas
Recipes for traditional Guyanese Christmas favorites are included here.

https://metemgee.com
This site features Guyanese recipes photographed step by step.

METEMGEE

This Guyanese stew is typically made from tuberous root vegetables cooked in peppery coconut milk. It's topped with dumplings called duff, and also usually served with fried fish filets.

2 tablespoons of coconut oil
1 medium yellow onion, chopped
4 cloves of garlic, finely chopped
2 scallions, chopped
1 12-ounce can, or 1½ cups (350 milliliters) coconut milk
3 cups (700 mL) water (or more coconut milk)
2 cassavas (yucas), peeled and cut into 3-inch (7.6-centimeter) pieces (if unavailable, substitute waxy white potatoes)
2 large sweet potatoes (orange or white), peeled, cut into 3-inch (7.6 cm) pieces
2 semi-ripe plantains, peeled, cut into 3-inch (7.6 cm) pieces
1 scotch bonnet, or other small, hot pepper, finely chopped
About 5 sprigs of fresh thyme or 1 teaspoon dried thyme
Salt, black pepper to taste
Optional trimmings: dumplings (duff); hard-boiled eggs, shelled and halved; fried fish filets (your own recipe)

In a large pot, heat coconut oil over a medium flame. Add the onions and cook until soft but not brown, about 4 minutes. Add the garlic and scallions and cook for 1 minute. Add the coconut milk, water, the pepper, and seasonings. Then, add the cassava and boil on high heat until the cassava is cooked and tender. (If substituting potatoes, skip this step and add them with the other vegetables.) Add the remaining vegetables. Add additional coconut milk or water if necessary to just barely cover the vegetables. Bring to a boil, turn down the heat, and cover. Simmer until vegetables can be easily pierced with a fork, but are not falling apart.

Drop spoonfuls of duff dough, if using, onto the stew; cover and let steam on medium heat for 10-15 minutes, or until cooked through.

Add trimmings to top of the stew, sprinkle with fresh thyme, and serve.

GUYANESE COCONUT ROCK BUNS

2 cups (240 grams) all-purpose flour
1 teaspoon grated orange zest
½ cup (120 g) butter, cut into small pieces
¼ cup (50 g) brown sugar
¼ cup (50 g) white sugar
½ tsp salt
½ tsp nutmeg
¼ cup (40 g) raisins (optional)
½ cup (50g) coconut flakes
1½ teaspoons baking powder
2 large eggs
1 teaspoons vanilla
Demerara sugar

Preheat oven to 400°F (200°C). Cover a baking sheet with parchment paper.

In a medium bowl, whisk together the flour, sugar, baking powder, grated orange, nutmeg, and salt. Work in the butter with a pastry blender or two knives, just until the mixture is unevenly crumbly. Stir in the raisins, if using, and coconut flakes.

In a separate bowl, whisk together the eggs and vanilla.

Gently fold the wet ingredients into the dry ingredients and stir until all is moistened and holds together like a ball.

Place dough on a floured surface and gently knead, folding dough over on itself about five times. Press out the dough to even thickness.

Shape into eight or ten "rocks" or use a cookie cutter. Sprinkle with Demerara sugar.

Place on a baking sheet.

Bake for 12-15 minutes or until lightly browned. Remove, let them cool, and serve.

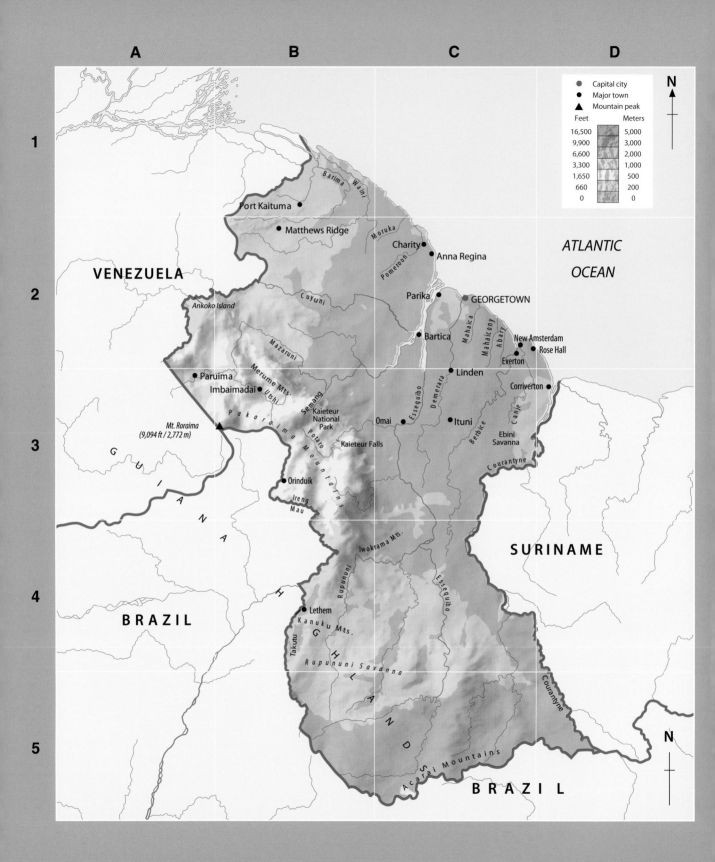

MAP OF GUYANA

Abary River, C2
Acarai Mountains, C5
Ankoko Island, A2
Anna Regina, C2
Atlantic Ocean, D1—D2

Barima River, B1
Bartica, C2
Berbice River, C3
Brazil, A3—A5, B3—B5, C5, D5

Canje River, C3
Charity, C2
Corriverton, D3
Courantyne River, C3—C4, D4—D5
Cuyuni River, B2

Demerara River, C3

Ebini Savanna, C3
Essequibo River, C3—C4
Everton, C2

Georgetown, C2
Guiana Highlands, A3, B4, C5

Imbaimadai, B3
Ireng River, B3
Ituni, C3

Iwokrama Mountains, B4, C4

Kaieteur Falls, B3
Kaieteur National Park, B3
Kanuku Mountains, B4

Lethem, B4
Linden, C3

Mahaica River, C2
Mahaicony River, C2
Matthews Ridge, B2
Mau River, B3
Mazaruni River, B2
Merume Mountains, B3
Moruka River, C2

New Amsterdam, C2

Omai, C3
Orinduik, B3

Pakaraima Mountains, B3
Parika, C2
Paruima, A3
Pomeroon River, C2
Port Kaituma, B1
Potaro River, B3

Roraima, Mount, B3
Rose Hall, C2
Rupununi River, B4
Rupununi Savanna, B4, C5

Semang River, B3
Suriname, C3—C4, D3—D5

Takutu River, B4

Utshi River, B3

Venezuela, A1—A4, B1—B3

Waini River, B1

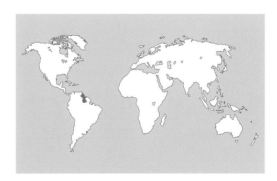

ECONOMIC GUYANA

Services

 Airports

 Ports

 Tourism

Manufacturing

 Food processing

 Meat packing

 Metalworking

 Sawmill, lumber, and wood products

 Sugar milling

Agriculture

 Cattle

 Coconut

 Rice

 Sugar

Natural Resources

 Bauxite

 Diamonds

 Fishing

 Gold

ABOUT THE ECONOMY

All figures are 2017 estimates unless otherwise noted.

GROSS DOMESTIC PRODUCT (GDP)
$3.628 billion

GDP GROWTH
2.1 percent

GDP PER CAPITA
$8,200

INFLATION RATE
2.1 percent

CURRENCY
Guyanaese dollar (GYD)
US $1 = GYD 209.02 (October 2018)

LABOR FORCE
320,000

UNEMPLOYMENT RATE
12 percent

POPULATION BELOW POVERTY LINE
43 percent (2013)

NATURAL RESOURCES
Bauxite, gold, diamonds, hardwood timber, shrimp, fish

AGRICULTURAL PRODUCTS
Sugarcane, rice, shrimp, fish, edible oils, beef, pork, poultry

INDUSTRIES
Bauxite, sugar, rice milling, timber, textiles, gold mining

MAJOR EXPORTS
Sugar, gold, bauxite, alumina, rice, shrimp, molasses, rum, timber

MAJOR IMPORTS
Manufactures, machinery, petroleum, food

MAIN TRADE PARTNERS
Export partners: Canada, United States, Panama, United Kingdom, Jamaica, Trinidad and Tobago
Import partners: Trinidad and Tobago, United States, China, Suriname

CULTURAL GUYANA

Shell Beach
The beach stretches for 90 miles (140 km) along Guyana's northwestern shore, between the Pomeroon and Waini Rivers. Four of the world's eight turtle species, including olive ridleys, hawksbills, and magnificent giant leatherbacks, struggle ashore at night to dig nests between March and July. Each lays as many as ten dozen eggs among numerous shells before returning to the Atlantic waters. These turtles used to be slaughtered for their meat and eggs but are now protected under a nongovernment conservation program.

Stabroek Market
The Stabroek Market houses 80,000 square feet (7,432 sq m) of stalls that sell items from household goods and gold jewelry to fresh meat and vegetables. Its nineteenth-century cast-iron clock tower can be seen for miles around and is a famous landmark.

Mount Roraima
Mount Roraima is the highest point in Guyana at 9,094 feet (2,772 m). Located in the Guiana Highlands at the point where the boundaries of Brazil, Venezuela, and Guyana meet, it is the source of many rivers of Guyana, and of the Amazon and Orinoco river systems. The Amerindians call it a mesa because of its giant flat top.

Cathedral of Saint George
The capital has a spacious, village atmosphere as buildings are mostly two-story wooden houses, all standing separately. The tallest wooden church building in the world is the Anglican Cathedral of Saint George, which was designed by Sir Arthur Bloomfield and consecrated in 1892.

Sea Wall
The flat coastal strip along the Atlantic coast was built up from centuries of sediment accumulation from the large South American rivers. It occupies an area of 6,486 square miles (16,800 sq km) and is below sea level by about 6.5 feet (2 m). The low concrete sea wall lines the coast of Guyana to protect Georgetown from the Atlantic Ocean. Colorful advertisements and political slogans cover the walls. On Sundays, crowds gather here to relax.

Kaieteur Falls
Located on the Potaro River within the Kaieteur National Park, Kaieteur Falls is accessible by road, river, or flight. Water initially tumbles 741 feet (226 m) over the edge of a sandstone plateau, then a further drop of 81 feet (25 m) over the great rocks at the bottom, making it the highest single-drop waterfall in the world. A rainbow arches eternally over the mist-covered boulders of the gorge.

Rupununi Savanna
The Kanuku Mountains divide this vast area of dry grasslands, with sparse trees, tall termite mounds, and wooded hills into the North and South Rupununi. Local *vaqueros* (cowboys) run large cattle ranges that date from the nineteenth century. Scattered Amerindian villages; a rich variety of wildlife species; colorful exotic bird species; and the world's largest water lilies, the *Victoria amazonica*, are common sights. Water tours by boat are conducted when the rains flood the savanna.

Iwokrama Forest
The Iwokrama is one of four pristine tropical forests remaining in the world. Rain forest flora and wildlife can be observed from the Canopy Walkway, a 505-foot (154 m) network of suspension bridges and decks. The Iwokrama is home to the highest number of fish and bat species in the world. It is also a living laboratory for sustainable tropical forest management.

ABOUT THE CULTURE

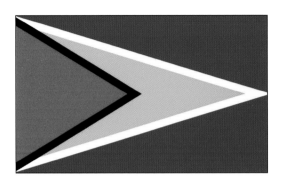

All figures are 2017 estimates, unless otherwise noted.

OFFICIAL NAME
Cooperative Republic of Guyana

LAND AREA
17,462 square miles (45,226 sq km)

CAPITAL
Georgetown, population 110,000 (2018)

POPULATION
737,718

URBANIZATION
urban population: 26.6 percent of total population (2018)

ETHNIC GROUPS
East Indian 39.8 percent, African 29.3 percent, mixed 19.9 percent, Amerindian 10.5 percent, others 0.5 percent (includes Portuguese, Chinese, white)

RELIGIONS
Protestant 34.8 percent, Hindu 24.8 percent, Roman Catholic 7.1 percent, Muslim 6.8 percent, Jehovah's Witness 1.3 percent, Rastafarian 0.5 percent, other Christian 20.8 percent, other 0.9 percent, none 3.1 percent (2012)

MAIN LANGUAGES
English (official), Guyanese Creole, Amerindian languages (including Carib and Arawak languages), Indian languages (including Caribbean Hindustani, a dialect of Hindi), Chinese (2014)

LIFE EXPECTANCY AT BIRTH
Total population: 68.6 years
Male: 65.6 years
Female: 71.8 years

BIRTHRATE
15.4 births per 1,000 population

DEATH RATE
7.4 deaths per 1,000 population

INFANT MORTALITY RATE
30.4 deaths per 1,000 live births

LITERACY RATE
Total population: 88.5 percent
Male: 87.2 percent
Female: 89.8 percent (2015)

TIMELINE

IN GUYANA	IN THE WORLD
	1492
	Christopher Columbus arrives in America.
1498	**1506**
Christopher Columbus sights Guyana.	Portuguese control east African coast.
1580	**1603**
Dutch establish trading posts up Essequibo River.	End of Elizabeth I's reign as Queen of England.
1620	**1620**
The Dutch West India Company imports slaves from Africa for sugarcane plantations.	Pilgrims sail the *Mayflower* to America.
1780–1813	**1776**
Guyana changes hands among the Dutch, French, and British.	US Declaration of Independence.
	1789–1799
	The French Revolution.
1879	**1861**
Gold is discovered in Guyana.	The US Civil War begins.
1889–1899	
Venezuela claims a large portion of Guyana west of the Essequibo River.	**1914**
	World War I begins.
1950	**1939**
Cheddi Jagan founds the Progressive People's Party (PPP).	World War II begins.
1953	
Britain suspends Guyana's constitution after PPP wins parliamentary election.	
1957	**1957**
PPP splits along racial lines.	Ghana becomes the first African
1961	country to win independence.
Guyana granted full autonomy; Cheddi Jagan (PPP) becomes prime minister.	
1962	
Venezuela revives territorial claims.	
1966	**1966**
Guyana is granted independence with Forbes Burnham as prime minister.	The Chinese Cultural Revolution.
1978	**1969**
Cult commits mass suicide at Jonestown.	US astronauts land on the moon.

IN GUYANA	IN THE WORLD
1980	
Guyana gets a new constitution, and Burnham becomes Guyana's first executive president.	
1985	
Desmond Hoyte (PNC) becomes president following the death of Burnham.	**1986** Nuclear power disaster at Chernobyl in Ukraine.
	1991 Breakup of the Soviet Union.
1992	
Cheddi Jagan (PPP) is elected president.	
1997	**1997** Hong Kong is returned to China.
President Jagan dies; is replaced by wife.	
1998	
Violent racial riots in Georgetown	
1999	
Bharrat Jagdeo becomes president after Janet Jagan resigns.	**2001** Terrorists attack the US on 9/11.
2006	
President Bharrat Jagdeo is reelected.	
2007	
UN tribunal brokers Guyana-Suriname border dispute.	**2008** US elects first African American president, Barack Obama.
	2009 Outbreak of H1N1 flu around the world.
2011	
Donald Ramotar is elected as president.	
2014	
Ramotar suspends opposition-dominated parliament.	
2015	**2015–2016** ISIS launches terror attacks in Belgium and France.
David Granger becomes president, ending twenty-three years of rule by Indian-dominated PPP. ExxonMobil announces "significant" oil discovery off the coast of Guyana.	**2017** Donald Trump becomes US president. Hurricanes devastate Houston, Caribbean islands, and Puerto Rico.
2018	**2018** Winter Olympics in South Korea.
Granger is diagnosed with lymphoma. UN refers Guyana-Venezuela land dispute to the International Court of Justice.	

GLOSSARY

Anansi
A spider trickster god who is popular in African tribal folklore.

arapaima (ah-rah-PAI-mah)
A very large freshwater fish

bragga **(BRAH-gah)**
A small Portuguese guitar.

callalu **(kah-lah-LOO)**
A soup combining ingredients from land and sea and eaten as a main course.

capybara
The world's largest rodent—also known as the water pig.

creole
A type of language based on two or more other languages.

cumfa **(KUM-fah)**
A quasi-religious African dance accompanied by drumming.

jalousie
A system of louvered boards in Guyanese housing design that can be angled differently to allow air to circulate.

jhag **(JAHG)**
A Hindu family thanksgiving, celebrated with religious talks, singing, and feasting.

Kali Mai Puja
An alternative healing practice in Guyana.

kathak **(KAH-tahk)**
A traditional East Indian dance performed by women.

negritude
A focus on the contributions of black writers, artists, and thinkers.

pandit
Hindu religious expert.

pork-knockers
Men who spend their lives looking for gold and diamonds in Guyana's interior.

que-que **(kwe-kwe)**
An African dance performed at weddings and other public celebrations.

rajao **(rah-JOWZ)**
A Portuguese banjo.

shirt-jac
Guyanese version of formal dress for men.

sitar
A stringed East Indian musical instrument.

varna (VAHR-nah)
One of four groups into which a soul is classified according to religious purity in Hinduism.

FOR FURTHER INFORMATION

BOOKS

Bahadur, Gaiutra. *Coolie Woman: The Odyssey of Indenture*. Chicago: The University of Chicago Press, 2014.

Smock, Kirk. *Guyana*. Chalfont St. Peter: Bradt Travel Guides, 2018.

WEBSITES

BBC News. Guyana country profile. https://www.bbc.com/news/world-latin-america-19546909

CIA World Factbook. Guyana. https://www.cia.gov/library/publications/the-world-factbook/geos/gy.html

Encyclopaedia Britannica. Guyana. https://www.britannica.com/place/Guyana

Freedom House. Guyana profile. https://freedomhouse.org/report/freedom-world/2018/guyana

Lonely Planet. Guyana. https://www.lonelyplanet.com/the-guianas/guyana

Parliament of the Cooperative Republic of Guyana. http://parliament.gov.gy

New York Times. Guyana. https://www.nytimes.com/topic/destination/guyana

FILMS

Jagessar, Rohit. *Guiana 1838*. RBC Radio, 2004.

Wasserman, Suzanne. *Thunder in Guyana*. Independent Lens, 2003.

MUSIC

Ring Play & Queh Queh Songs of Guyana. Marlon Jardine. Amerindian, 2009.

Traditional African Ritual Music of Guyana. Folkways Records, 1982

BIBLIOGRAPHY

Burke, Mercilin M. "Climate Change and Its Effects On Guyana." *Guyana Chronicle*, September 17, 2017. http://guyanachronicle.com/2017/09/17/climate-change-and-its-effects-on-guyana.

Encyclopaedia Britannica. "Guyana." https://www.britannica.com/place/Guyana.

Donley, Arvin. "Guyana Increases Rice Production, Exports." World-Grain.com, August 23, 2018. https://www.world-grain.com/articles/10869-guyana-increases-rice-production-exports.

Durant, Nigel. "Easter: Kite Flying in Guyana." *Guyanese Online*. April 20, 2014. https://guyaneseonline.net/2014/04/20/easter-kite-flying-in-guyana-with-pictures-by-nigel-durant.

Guyana Chronicle. http://guyanachronicle.com.

Kaieteur News. https://www.kaieteurnewsonline.com.

Krauss, Clifford. "The $20 Billion Question for Guyana." *New York Times*, July 20, 2018. https://www.nytimes.com/2018/07/20/business/energy-environment/the-20-billion-question-for-guyana.html.

Laville, Sandra. "Guyanese Campaigners Mount Legal Challenge Against Three Oil Giants." *Guardian*, March 22, 2018. https://www.theguardian.com/environment/2018/mar/22/guyanese-campaigners-mount-legal-challenge-against-three-oil-giants.

Lonely Planet. "Guyana." https://www.lonelyplanet.com/the-guianas/guyana.

Maidenberg, Micah, and Manuela Andreoni. "The Country That Wasn't Ready to Win the Lottery." *Foreign Policy*, June 19, 2018. https://foreignpolicy.com/2018/06/19/the-country-that-wasnt-ready-to-win-the-lottery-guyana-oil.

Noel, Melissa. "Guyana Jubilee: Celebrating 50 Years of Independence." ABC News, May 27, 2016. https://www.nbcnews.com/news/nbcblk/guyana-independence-n581606.

Worldfolio, The. "Guyana Budgets on Better Education." 2016. http://www.theworldfolio.com/news/guyana-budgets-on-better-education/4199.

Youkee, Mat. "Guyana's Border Towns Threatened by Violent Gangs as Venezuela Crisis Deepens." *Guardian*, August 2, 2018. https://www.theguardian.com/world/2018/aug/02/venezuela-crisis-violence-guyana-border.

INDEX

abuse, 26, 68

Africa, 15, 27, 63, 67, 93, 110—111, 127

African, 6—7, 26, 28, 61—63, 71, 89—91, 98—99, 107, 111, 122, 125, 127

Afro-Guyanese, 6, 30, 32, 35, 62—64, 68, 71—72, 78, 83, 89, 92, 100, 107, 114

Amerindians, 6, 23, 25—26, 56, 61—64, 67, 85, 87, 89, 98, 104, 110

Anansi, 93

animals, 15, 17—18, 56, 58, 87, 89, 103—104, 106

Atlantic, 6, 11—13, 16, 51, 54—55, 98, 107

Awacaipu, 85, 87, 89

bauxite, 6, 12, 21, 40, 43—44, 46—49, 52, 63

Berbice, 14, 21, 24, 26, 28, 46, 48, 67, 98—99

Booker's Guiana, 29

Brazil, 5, 11—12, 14—15, 18, 65, 95—96, 102

Britain, 11, 26, 29—32, 35, 38, 67, 115, 117

British, 5, 15, 20, 26, 28—30, 37, 39—40, 43, 61, 67—69, 83, 95, 98, 103, 111, 113, 115—116, 122

British Guiana, 5, 28—30, 37, 69, 83

Burnham, Forbes, 30—31, 35—36, 39, 41, 43—44, 67, 69, 77, 90—92, 100

Caribbean, 6, 20, 28—29, 32, 39, 45, 49, 57, 67, 69, 72, 77—78, 93, 95—96, 99, 103, 107, 110, 115—116, 119, 122—123, 125, 127

CARICOM, 45, 48, 122—123

cassava, 23, 125—127, 130

Catholic Standard, the, 92, 100

children, 63, 72—73, 77, 84, 90, 93—94, 100, 115—116, 120, 128

Christian/Christians, 83, 87, 92, 119, 120

Christianity, 64, 85, 89, 122

climate, 16, 51, 54—56, 59, 105—106

climate change, 51, 54—56, 59

coconut buns (recipe), 133

coconuts, 127, 130—131

colonial/colony, 5, 6, 20, 23, 24—25, 27—30, 35, 51, 61, 67, 71, 72, 83, 95, 98, 103, 105—106, 110—111, 116, 122

constitution, 31, 35—36, 41, 91, 121

creole, 63, 72—73, 76, 95—96, 98—101, 125

cricket, 77, 86, 112—113, 115—116

Cuffy, 26, 67

cults, 23, 83, 90—92, 100

Demerara River, 20—22, 24

diamonds, 6, 12, 25, 38, 40, 52, 78

Dutch, the, 20—21, 24—27, 30, 67, 95, 97—99, 128

elections, 6—7, 30—32, 35—36, 39, 100, 111

Essequibo, 14, 24, 26, 33, 40, 46, 48—49, 55, 58, 67, 99, 120

Europe, 25, 45, 67, 105

ExxonMobil, 8, 53, 59

Five Pillars of Faith (Islam), 88

flooding/floods, 16, 18, 32, 51, 55, 104, 106

forests, 5, 10—13, 18, 24, 38, 46, 48, 51—53, 55—59, 65, 97, 105

Georgetown, 11, 14, 20—22, 32, 34, 39, 46, 48—49, 51, 58, 62—63, 66—67, 70, 76—77, 82—86, 88, 98, 105—107, 112—115, 118, 120, 122, 124, 128—129

gold, 6, 12, 14, 25, 37, 40, 43—45, 47—48, 52, 75, 78, 109

Granger, David A., 7, 32—33, 35

Guianas, the, 11, 23—25, 95—96, 99

Hallelujah Church, 87, 107

Hindus, 70—71, 73—75, 80, 85—87, 91, 115, 119—120

House of Israel, 91—93, 100

indentured laborers, 6, 27—29, 61, 63, 65, 72, 108, 120

independence, 5, 23, 29, 31—32, 35—36, 40, 68, 77, 79, 83, 104, 119, 122—123

India, 6, 27—29, 63, 72, 84, 87, 89, 120

INDEX

Indians, 30, 61—63, 68, 72—73, 75, 80, 83—84, 86, 97, 99, 103, 107—109, 115, 121, 125, 127
indigenous, 13—15, 17, 20, 23, 25, 38, 55—56, 62, 64—65, 85, 89, 96, 103
Indo-Guyanese, 6, 27, 32, 35, 37, 62—63, 68, 72—73, 78, 87, 92, 99, 107, 114

Jagan, Cheddi, 30—32, 37, 49, 104
Jagan, Janet, 31—32, 37
Jones, Jim, 90—91, 93
Jonestown massacre, 33, 90

Kaieteur Falls, 13, 21
Kali, 80—81

Makushí people, 64, 87, 99
metemgee, 125, 127, 130 (recipe)
mining, 38, 43, 44, 46—48, 51—53, 57—58
Muslims, 71, 73, 83, 87—89, 119, 121—122

Obeah, 89
oil, 8, 33, 40, 43, 53, 59, 76, 130

plantations, 26, 28—30, 55, 63, 67, 71—72, 99
PNC, 7, 30—32, 35, 68, 77, 92, 100
pollution, 51—52, 54, 114
pork-knockers, 78
Portuguese, 25, 28—29, 31, 61—65, 68, 97, 106, 127
poverty, 5, 7, 27, 51, 65, 72, 79
PPP, 6, 30—32, 35, 37, 68, 92, 100
president 7, 31—33, 35—37, 39, 43, 90

rain forests, 5, 10, 11, 46, 53, 56—57, 59
Raleigh, Sir Walter, 24—25
rice, 6, 12, 30, 38, 43, 45—46, 48, 54—55, 75, 125, 127—128
rivers, 5, 6, 10—15, 17—22, 24, 38, 40, 46—48, 51—54, 56—58, 64—65, 78, 89, 96—97, 103, 105, 114, 120
Rodney, Walter, 67, 69, 92, 111
Roraima, 14—15, 21, 25, 40, 49, 64, 85, 98, 110

Saint George's Cathedral, 83
schools, 77—78, 84—85, 87, 115, 116, 128
slaves, 6, 25—28, 30, 62—64, 67, 71—72, 84, 86, 93, 99, 111, 122
South America, 5, 15, 79, 95—96, 124
Stabroek, 62, 98, 101, 114, 124, 128—129
sugar cane, 6, 27
suicide, 23, 79, 81, 85, 90—91
Suriname, 5, 11—12, 23, 33, 48

United Nations, 40
United States, 32, 40, 46, 48, 69, 78—79, 91, 101

Venezuela, 5, 8, 11—12, 14—15, 18, 33, 40—41, 64—65, 95—96
violence, 79

waterfalls, 6, 11, 13—15, 19, 25, 51, 89
wildlife, 6, 17, 21, 53, 56, 94
women, 31, 63, 71—72, 74, 89, 108, 114, 125